English Grammar Simplifier

Kotra Siva Rama Krishna

Published by Kotra Siva Rama Krishna, 2023.

While every precaution has been taken in the preparation of this book, the publisher assumes no responsibility for errors or omissions, or for damages resulting from the use of the information contained herein.

ENGLISH GRAMMAR SIMPLIFIER

First edition. January 25, 2023.

Copyright © 2023 Kotra Siva Rama Krishna.

ISBN: 979-8215035184

Written by Kotra Siva Rama Krishna.

Also by Kotra Siva Rama Krishna

Two Strangers On The Bed
A Girl's Conflict
Enna
Strawberry
Dusk
Just Relax!
Delicious Predicament
Nirupama
Half Opened Doors
Lovenest
Moonshine
Scarecrow
Closed Doors
Disturbed
Handfuls of Sand
Mansion of Illusions
Rain Flower
Rose Garden
Sand Dunes
Snow Flower
Split Personality
Being Possessed
Objection Sustained
House of Delusions
Rustle in the Leaves

Sasikala
Amaswitha
English Grammar Simplifier
Wisps of Smoke
Shadow in the Mirror
Love is Dangerous with a Stranger
Shadow of a Spirit
Unwanted Guests
Broken Window
Loud Thunder Nearby
Spirit in the Mirror
Whispers in the Night
Shadows in the Twilight
Twisted Shadow
Body, Mind and You
Summer Holidays
Flower of the Mist
Nail Polish
Laughter of a Spirit
Lipstick
Flickering Shadow
Dancing Shadow

Table of Contents

Edition License Notes

This ebook/paper back/hard cover is licensed for your personal enjoyment only. This ebook/paper back/hard cover may not be re-sold or given away to other people. If you would like to share this ebook/paper back/hard cover with another person, please ask them to purchase an additional copy for each recipient. If you're reading this ebook/paper back/hard cover and did not purchase it, or it was not purchased for your enjoyment only, then please return to the publisher or your favorite retailer and purchase your own copy. Thank you for respecting the hard work of this author.

Indemnity Clause

This book has been written after thorough research and consultation of several other English grammar books. But if there are any mistakes either verbally, grammatically or otherwise crept into this book, it is without this writer's intention or knowledge and this writer is not going to be responsible for the same. Readers are advised to go through other standard English grammar books also to update and conform their English grammar.

Writer's Word

I have written this English grammar book keeping in view particularly all those who want to get a grip on English grammar. This book has not covered each and everything in English grammar and it is not exhaustive! But this book sure does give an understanding of English grammar. This book surely will be quite helpful to all those who want to elevate their English language standard and develop their English grammar skills. Even I have consulted several other grammar books on English while writing this book, the definitions, examples, etc. in this English grammar book are completely my own. I have used the other grammar books only for complete understanding of English grammar. I have taken every care to give correct information on English grammar. Still if you come across any grammatical mistakes, verbal mistakes or otherwise in this book please let me know, I shall correct the same in my next edition

Writer's Small Request

It would be a big irony that if grammatical mistakes, verbal mistakes or other incongruities do happen in a grammar book. But despite my diligence and revision, I am afraid that there may be grammatical mistakes, verbal mistakes or other mistakes or incongruities in this book. Whichever such things you may come across while going through this grammar book, please let me know and I correct the same in my next edition.

About The Writer

The writer is an Indian English writer and Post-Graduate in English who writes mostly fiction books and so far he has written forty seven books out of which forty five books are romantic, psychological thrillers and the remaining two are non-fiction books, Body, Mind and You and English Grammar Simplifier. The word count of his books range from 15,000 to 3,50,000 and the total word count of all his books is more than 40,00,000 (Forty Lakhs Words). All his books are available as ebooks and paperbacks and can be found by searching with the name 'Kotra Siva Rama Krishna':

Dedication

I am dedicating this book to my Lord Sri Sri Sri Raja Gopala Swamy at Kailasapatnam who saves our family all the time, who guides me all the time, who helps me all the time.

Sentence

A sentence is a group of words. Sentences are used to convey something. Words make only partial sense and no sense some times. To make sense, words have to be put in a row. To make meaningful sense, words have to be put in an order in that row. Why is that order? Just observe the following sentence.

'Could he as fast as Mike ran in that running'

Is the above sentence making any sense at all? Of course, the above sentence is making sense but not in a proper and complete way. To give proper and complete sense, words need to be used in an order. Grammar tells us about the order and it has some rules also to make the language properly understandable to one and all.

Now, observe the following sentence:

In that running race, Mike ran as fast as he could

The above sentence is perfectly understandable to everyone. So, to make sentences understandable to all and to convey the meaning of it in a proper way we have to use grammar. Now is the time that we have to start discussing about that grammar.

So far, we learnt that sentences consist words. Those words need to be put in an order and that order governs by grammar. The words in sentences are called by specific names also.

The general rule that should be followed while making a sentence is, it should begin with a capital letter and "." should be put at the end of the sentence. If the sentence is big we can use ',' in between the sentence to break it to make it easy to read and understand. Any number of "," can be used in a sentence to make it easily understandable.

Anyhow it can be said that there are four types of sentences. They are (1) Declarative (2) Interrogative (3) Imperative and (4) Exclamatory. The uses of these sentences are as follows:

<u>Declarative Sentence:</u>

You can know the use of it by observing the meaning of the words. These sentences simply declare something. They simply tell the state, being or nature of something. Observe the following examples.

1) Nath is a tall boy.

2) Lata is a clever girl

3) This book is very good to read.

Sentences that tell about the facts or truths also called as 'declarative sentences'.

1) Sun rises in the east

2) Earth is round.

<u>Interrogative sentence:</u>

You guessed it right! Yes, sentences that are used to ask questions are called as interrogative sentences.

1) Where did you put the grammar book?

2) At what time Lata comes here?

A question mark "?" should be put at the end of a sentence

<u>Imperative sentence:</u>

Sentences that are used to express commands, requests and desires are called as imperative sentences.

1) Go there and sit straight! (command)

2) Please give me that book. (request)

3) I want to have an apple now. (desire)

<u>Exclamatory sentence:</u>

Exclamatory sentences are used to express strong sudden feelings, surprise and shock! Unlike other sentences, you have to put '!' at the end of these sentences.

1) How beautiful she is!

2) It burst in an unexpected way!

3) Doing that is a most challenging thing in the world!

Subject, Verb and Object

It can be said that there are three important parts in a sentence. They are subject, verb and object. Observe the following sentence.

Nath threw the ball.

In the above sentence

– the subject is – Nath

-the verb is – threw

-the object is –ball

Verb is called as predicate also. This verb may be sometimes a single word and sometimes more than a single word also.

While expressing orders or requests subject can be omitted. That means subject is understood. Subject does not feel offensive to move away in such situations.

Go there. Here the subject 'you' is understood.

Give me that pen. Here also the subject 'you' is understood.

Another simple thing that has to be understood is; only 'you' has the great heart to disappear like that but not all the pronouns. We cannot omit the other necessary pronouns as subjects and make sentences.

Sometimes sentences can be made without objects also. Here not just omitting, there will be no objects at all. No offence to any pronoun.

She smiles beautifully.

He walks slowly.

Sentences made with intransitive verbs don't need an object. It is too early to discuss about intransitive verbs here and you can know about them in an appropriate place.

Parts of Speech

Noun, Pronoun, Verb, Adverb, Adjective, Preposition, Conjunction, Interjection.

These words are called Parts of Speech. I think it came from parts in speech, what we talk. Anyhow, this Parts of Speech governs the whole grammar.

Now we shall discuss about each Parts Of Speech as much as possible

Noun

Nouns are the words used for places, persons or things.

Places: deserts, forests, playgrounds, etc.

Persons: old man, young-man, boy, woman, child, etc.

Things: bitterness, cold, kindness, stone, gold, etc.

It is not over yet. Nouns are not as simple as just the above. We have to discuss a lot about them. According to their nature, nouns have been divided into following categories.

Proper noun:

Proper nouns are not just places, persons or things. Only those which meant a particular place, person or thing can be called as a Proper Noun.

Himalayas, Mexico, America, Williams, Rose

In the above, Himalayas, Mexico, America, are particular names of places and Williams, Rose are particular names of persons. Just like that!

I am thinking it is better to say something important about Proper Noun here itself. A Proper Noun should always be started with a capital letter!

Common noun:

If you understand the meaning of the words of it, you understand what it is. 'Common' in persons, places or things. The same kind of places, the same kind of persons and the same kind of things are called as common nouns. The following are the examples for Common Nouns.

Woman, child, adult, school, college, principal, teacher.

<u>Collective noun:</u>

Group of persons, places and things are called as Collective Nouns. Collection means a group. Meaning in the word itself!

Teachers, boys, stones, girls

<u>Abstract noun:</u>

Don't break your head to know the meaning of it in the word 'abstract.' You may if you see all the synonyms to 'abstract' but will be little confusing. I give a little explanation.

All the things that can only be thought of, but cannot be touched.

The *kindness* in your uncle is so great, he gives you hundred rupees every time he visits your house.

You can feel the *'kindness'* of your uncle but you cannot touch it and keep it somewhere safe.

The *'harshness'* in your girlfriend makes you sick sometimes.

Here also you cannot touch the *'harshness'* in your girlfriend and throw it so far away that it never can be found.

It has not come to an end yet. All the names of arts, sciences and other studies are also called as abstract nouns. Why so? You can talk about some art, for example, painting but you cannot touch it. You can think about natural science but you cannot touch it.

How abstract nouns are formed? Just observe the following:

i) Abstract nouns can be derived from common nouns:

Womanhood from woman; manliness from man

ii) Abstract nouns can be derived from adjectives:

Foolishness from foolish; richness from rich

iii) Abstract nouns can be derived from verbs:

Prosperity from prosper

<u>Countable noun:</u>

You already understood I think. All the things that can be counted are called as Countable Nouns. We can cite innumerable examples

Stone, rod, person, doctor, teacher, etc.

To that matter Pronouns can be used as Countable Nouns also.

I am thinking it is better to reveal another important characteristic of Countable Nouns here itself. You can form plurals only to the Countable Nouns. Just see.

Stones, rods, persons, doctors, teachers, etc

Uncountable noun:

I know that your shrewd mind is guessing that there is something like this also after you came to know about countable nouns. Feel happy! Your guessing is right. All the things that cannot be counted are uncountable nouns.

Kindness, happiness, gold, silver, mathematics, physical science, etc.

Poor uncountable nouns have a disability. They don't have plurals!

All abstract nouns are uncountable. So, don't make plurals of abstract nouns.

There is a small exemption to this. Sometimes we can make plurals to uncountable nouns also.

Golds, silvers, kindnesses, like this. But the meaning shall be changed.

He has many golds with him- meaning, he has many gold coins with him.

The kindnesses of him are innumerable- meaning, the many number of times he acted with kindness.

Compound noun:

Compound nouns do have more than one word. Observe the following examples:

Brother-in-law

Sister-in-law

Commander-in-chief

If we want to make plurals of these words, we have to add 's' to the principal words of these nouns. Plurals of the above nouns are as follows:

Brothers-in-law

Sisters-in-law

Commanders-in-chief

Gender

There is a particular characteristic to the nouns. That is Gender. A noun can be feminine, masculine, common or neutral. Now we shall see how it can be.

<u>Feminine</u>

You understood it perfectly! Yes, it came from female and only living beings can be feminine (Is it is so? There is a small exemption here. We discuss it later.)

Woman, girl, doe, hind, tigress, etc.

<u>Masculine</u>

Once again you are right. It derived from male and only living beings can be male just like feminine (Sorry, a small exemption here also. Just wait, I promise I explain)

Man, boy, deer, lion, etc.

<u>Common</u>

However intelligent you may be you cannot say whether it is male or female just by looking at the word. Observe the examples.

Parent, child, pupil, servant, peon, enemy, etc.

Unless these are used in sentences you cannot know about their gender.

She is a wonderful parent!

He worked like a servant in their house.

She behaved like an enemy with me.

So the nouns which can be used either male or female are called as common nouns.

<u>Neuter</u>

Those things which cannot be either male or female. What things cannot be either male or female? You might have guessed this by now. All inanimate things come under neuter gender.

Stone, book, pen, pencil, etc.

Remember. I promised you to explain for what inanimate things feminine and masculine genders are used. They are not many. Just observe the following examples.

The *sea* roared like a lion. *He* wanted to engulf our boats with its tides.

Here *'sea'* is inanimate but we used masculine pronoun 'he' for it. Sometimes, for the inanimate things, which represent greatness, power, masculine (gender) pronoun would be used.

The *moon* is shining very bright in the sky, *her* rays are so cool and giving peace to the earth.

Here *'moon'* is inanimate but we used feminine pronoun *'her'* for it. Sometimes, for the inanimate things, which represent beauty, delicacy, love, kindness, feminine (gender) pronoun is used.

Alright, we shall now worry about number of the nouns

Number

Nouns whether they are personal, common or neutral, sometimes they also like company and want to be more than one. We shall see what it would be if there is only one and more than one.

<u>Singular</u>

Whether there is only one, persons or otherwise, it is called as singular. Observe the following examples.

Man, woman, pen, pencil.

The above things are only one and they are called as in *singular*. When there is only one thing that is said to be in *singular*.

<u>Plural:</u>

To get the status of plural, the persons or things, need to be more than one.

Men, women, books, pencils, etc.

Usually, plural nouns are formed by adding '**s**' to the singular noun like in the following examples.

Book (singular)

Books (plural)

Pen (singular)

Pens (plural)

It may be irritating to you but there are some exceptions to this simple rule of adding '*s*' to the singular noun to form plurals. The following examples make it clear to you.

Foot (singular)

Feet (plural)

Woman (singular)

Women (plural)

Man (singular)

Men (plural)

Tooth (singular)

Teeth (plural)

Don't ever try to form plurals of the above words by adding 's' to the singular. You will become great fun to the listeners then.

The words ending with *s, sh, ch, x, o* don't satisfy with single 's' and they demand for *'es'* to transform into plurals.

Branch (singular)

Branches (plural)

Match (singular)

Matches (plural)

Tax (singular)

Taxes (plural)

There are some words ending with *'y'* and these also demand for adding *'es'* to be transformed into plurals. But the ending letter *'y'* in these words does not like more company and just disappears making poor *'i'* stand in its place after *'es'* being added in the end to form plural from singular.

Baby (singular)

Babies (plural)

Lady (singular)

Ladies (plural)

Story (singular)

Stories (plurals)

You and I both wish a lot the varieties of forming plurals end atleast by now. But the makers of English grammar are heartless. There are some more varieties.

Words ending with *'f'* or *'fe'* also transform into plurals after adding *'es'* to them. But the *'f'* or *'fe'* in the ending of the word put *'v'* in their place before leaving the company of other letters in the word.

Loaf (singular)
Loaves (plural)
Wolf (singular)
Wolves (plural)
Knife (singular)
Knives (plural)
Life (singular)
Lives (plural)

Some words are more liberal and they can be transformed into plurals by adding either 's' or 'ves' to them. This means, you can transform them into plurals either by adding 's' to them or by adding 'ves' if you are willing to take more pain and you are having more literary interest.

Wharf (singular)
Wharfs (plural)
Wharves (plural)
Hoof (singular)
Hoofs (plural)
Hooves (plural)

If you think it is only 's', 'es' or 'ves' have the capacity to transform the singulars into plurals, you are wrong! There is another set of letters 'en' 'ren' which look at you angrily. Because, by taking 'en' 'ren' at the end of them, some words joyfully transform themselves into plurals.

Ox (singular)
Oxen (plural)
Child (singular)
Children (plural)

Some singular words have the same word for plural also. But they have a 'es' added plural also with a different meaning.

Fish (singular)
Fish (plural) used to denote more than one fish
Fishes (plural) different types of fishes.

Some singular words are rigid. They don't want to change themselves into plurals. Whether you like it or not you have to use the same word for plural also. Some of those adamant words are given hereunder

Swine, sheep, deer, cod, trout, salmon, aircraft

There are some other words. They hate to be singular and they want strength. You can use them only plural and there is no other way. The following are some of those.

Bellows, scissors, tongs, pincers, spectacles, jeans, tights, shorts, thanks, proceeds, tidings.

You have to use only plural verb after these words.: ***were, are, have, etc.***

There are some deceptive words. They appear like plural but in reality they are singular. Just observe the following and be careful with those types of words.

Mathematics, physics, electronics, mumps, measles, billiards

These words should be followed by a singular verb : ***was, is, has, etc.***

Some nouns, especially collective, so obedient and they don't want to be haughty. Even they are singular in form you have to use them only in plural.

Poultry, cattle, people

The ***poultry*** we have are not many.

The ***cattle*** are coming this way.

The ***people*** of that city are one lakh

These words should be followed by plural verb: ***were, are, have***, etc.

There are some compound nous, comprising more than one word. You have to add '*s*' to the principal word in them to form plural.

Son-in-law (singular)

Sons-in-law (plural)

Daughter-in-law (singular)

Daughters-in-law (plural)

Mother-in-law (singular)

Mothers-in-law (plural)

Some singular nouns do have two plurals and each plural does have a different type of meaning.

Index (singular)

Indexes (plural): tables of contents to books

Indices (plural): signs used in algebra.

Cloth (singular)

Cloths (plural): kinds or pieces of cloth.

Clothes (plural): garments.

Here is a caution to you. Abstract nouns and proper nouns cannot be formed into plural. They have to be used only in singular always

Now you are going to be introduced to another important aspect of nouns. That is case.

Case

Before we discuss any more about noun cases we have to know some important aspects of a sentence.

Stuart threw the stone

The above sentence contains three main parts 'Stuart' 'threw' 'the stone'

Stuart- is the subject of the sentence

Threw-is the verb of the sentence

The stone – is the object of the sentence

By this it can be pretty easily understood that a sentence contains three important parts, subject, verb, object.

Nominative Case

The noun (or pronoun) in the place of the subject is said to be in Nominative Case. In the above sentence 'Stuart' is in Nominative Case. The other examples for Nominative Case.

She hit the dog. (Here 'she' being the subject is said to be in Nominative Case)

He gave a coin. (Here 'he' being the subject is said to be in Nominative Case)

Objective Case

The noun or pronoun in the place of the object is said to be in objective case. Or you may say it is in Accusative Case and it takes no offence. In the first referred sentence 'Stuart threw the stone' *the stone* is in Accusative Case. We can cite the above examples for Objective Case also.

She hit the dog. (Here 'the dog' being the object is said to be in Objective Case)

He gave a coin. (Here 'a coin' being the object is said to be in Objective Case)

Some other important point regarding Objective Case. If a noun or to that matter a pronoun also follows a proposition, they become the objects of that pronoun and said to be in Objective Case. Observe the following examples.

She sat on the table. (Here 'the table' became the object of the proposition *'on'*)

He jumped over the wall (Here the wall became the object of the proposition *'over'*)

Dative Case

It may be a little confusing but not very much if you pay attention. Observing an example makes it easy to you to understand.

The teacher gave a pencil to Williams.

Here observe 'a pencil'. It is the indirect object to the verb gave. An indirect object is said to be in Dative Case. As such, here 'a pencil' is in Dative Case.

John threw ***the ball*** towards Michael.

She gave ***the banana*** to her daughter.

The doctor gave ***an injunction*** to the patient.

In the above three sentences ***'the ball'***, ***'the banana'*** and ***'an injunction'*** are said to be in Dative Case. Even though they are the indirect objects, they have the privilege to follow the verb immediately. But they are deprived of the facility to have a preposition before them. There should be no preposition before an indirect object.

Possessive (or Genitive) Case

This case may create a little more interest in you because this denotes possession or authority. Going through few examples before, makes the task easier.

It is my pen.

Michael's intelligence is more than Williams'

Our specimen is better than theirs

I did not see their example yet.

I am not going to bear your audacity anymore.

'It is my pen.' – Here *'my'* denotes possession of the pen. As such, *'my'* is said to be in Possessive Case.

Michael's intelligence is more than Williams' - Michael's and Williams' are said to be in Possessive Case. They are in possession of intelligence.

I did not see their example yet. – 'their example' the example made by them or set by them. The ownership, authority or possession of an example.

I am not going to bear 'your audacity' anymore. – the audacity possessed by someone.

Nouns are adamant and they don't change their form and the same noun should be used for nominative, dative, possessive and accusative case. But pronouns don't want to remain the same and change themselves from case to case.

She gave him the pen (Here 'she' is the subject and said to be in Nominative Case)

He gave her a slap on the cheek (Here 'her' is in the indirect object (Dative Case)

They never agreed to that (Here 'they' is subject of the sentence and said to be in Nominative Case)

It is agreeable to them. (Here 'them' is object of the sentence and said to be in Objective Case)

The pronouns do change their form in the following manner for nominative, dative and accusative cases.

<u>She</u>

Nominative – she

Dative – her

Possessive – her, hers

Objective – her

He

Nominative –he

Dative – him

Possessive – his

Objective – him

They

Nominative –they

Dative – them

Possessive – their

Objective – them

It is not very strictly followed but only personal pronouns have the authority to be used with possessive case.

My pen.

Her victory.

Their glory.

In the above three sentences 'my', 'her' and 'their' are said to be in possessive case.

Printer's cartridge conveys the same sense but ***cartridge of the printer*** is more proper

Book's cover conveys the same sense but ***cover of the book*** is more proper

Vocative Case

Be relaxed! Good news! It is the last of the noun's cases and the easiest one. The following examples prove how easy it is.

Williams, stand up on the bench.

You, come near to me.

Mr. Michael, why did not you attend the yesterday's class?

A noun or pronoun, which is called or addressed in a sentence, is said to be in vocative case. As such, in the above sentence, 'Williams', 'you' and 'Mr. Michael' are said to be in vocative case.

Nouns in apposition

A noun follows another noun to describe it is said to be Noun In Apposition.

Williams, the doctor, said that the patient is safe.

He, the village chief, has done a lot for the village.

She, Reema's mother, is an English teacher.

In the above examples, 'the doctor', 'the village chief' and 'Reema's mother' are Nouns In Apposition as they are describing the noun preceded them. The noteworthy point here is, the Nouns In Apposition should be in the same case of the noun they are describing.

Pronoun

We have discussed so far upto now about nouns. Next comes the pronouns. What are the pronouns and when and how we use them? Just like the Noun, Pronoun also is a long chapter. First I shall tell you in a simple way what the pronouns are:

Pronouns are those which we use in place of nouns to avoid repetition of nouns.

We use pronouns in place of nouns to avoid repetition of same nouns again and again. Using the same noun again and again in the same sentence may also convey the same meaning but appears awkward. Observe the following sentence.

Rony is a sweet girl. She wakes up early in the morning, attends her daily routine quickly, makes her prayers diligently, finishes her homework quickly and she goes to her school at the right time.

In the above first sentence Rony is a proper noun. In the second sentence it has been replaced with 'she' and 'her'. Replace 'she' and 'her' in the second sentence everywhere with Rony and see how it appears. It appears awkward.

When we use a personal pronoun in the place of a noun it should be in the same gender, number and person of that noun.

In the above example the personal pronouns 'she' and 'her' are in the same feminine gender, singular and in third person in accordance with the noun Rony.

When a personal pronoun follows a collective noun it must be in singular.

Observe the following examples:

The group *has* taken its vow in the ground.

The mob *lost* its grip on the villagers.

In the above examples the collective nouns *'the group'* and *'the mob'* followed by singular noun *'it.'*

If the persons or things comprised in the group are taken individually or separately, then a plural pronoun should follow it.

Observe the following example:

The members of the group divided themselves into several categories.

When two or more singular nouns connected by *'and'*, the pronoun followed must be in plural.

Examples:

He and she got their punishment.

Williams and Johnny went to their homes.

Here is an exception of course, if the two nouns connected by *'and'* refer to the same person, the pronoun must be in singular.

Example:

The class leader and school leader, Mr.Arbit, took his seat.

It has to be understood, Mr.Arbit, the same person, is the class leader and school leader also as such followed by singular pronoun *'his'*.

The headmaster of the school and postmaster of the village, Mrs.Aron Silky, took her diploma in mathematics.

It has to be understood that Mrs.Aron Silky is the headmaster and postmaster also as such followed by singular pronoun *'her.'*

If 'each' or 'every' preceded the nouns, even the nouns connected by 'and', the pronoun followed must be in singular.

Examples:

Each boy and each man in that room took his chair.

Each girl and each woman in that village has her share in the cooking.

When two or more singular nouns connected by or, either—-or, neither—-nor, the pronoun followed should be in singular.

Examples:

The man or the boy forgot his hat here.

Either the principal or the teacher has his role in the plot.

Neither Rakesh nor Arjun has his book here last night.

Neither Uma nor Lilli took her plate with them.

The exception to the above rule comes when the latter noun is in plural

Either the man or the crowd accompanied him did not remember their manners

Neither Uma nor the whole people in the kitchen took their plates with them.

The pronoun must be in plural, if a *singular* and *plural noun* connected by *'or'*, *'nor'* *'either ....or'* *'neither ......nor'* or *'and'*.

The *plural noun* should be used after the *singular noun*.

Either the man or the crowd accompanied him did not remember their manners

The teacher or the children forgot their books here

Neither the thief nor the villagers chasing him stopped their running.

The following are the personal pronouns:

I, you, he, she, it, (if it represents living beings), we, they, who

(i) When I heard the news, I felt so much happy.

(ii) We never heard such type of stories before.

(iii) You are right in what you have said. All you people are very good.

(iv) She is right in her thinking but he is wrong in his approach and they both need to sit together and settle the issue

Iv) He threw a stone and it hit the gate.

In the sentence (i) 'I' is the singular personal pronoun. It is also said to be in First Person Singular.

In the sentence (ii) 'we' is the plural personal pronoun. It is also said to be in First Person Plural.

In the first sentence (iii) 'you' is the singular personal pronoun. In the second sentence (iii) 'you' is the plural personal pronoun. It is also said to be in Second Person.

An important hint: 'you' also an adamant personal pronoun and does not allow any change from singular to plural. That means you have to use the same 'you' for singular and plural also.

In the beginning part of the sentence (iv) 'she' and 'he' are the singular personal pronouns. They are said to be in Third Person Singular.

In the later part of the sentence (iv), 'they' is plural personal pronoun. It is said to be in Third Person Plural.

From the above it can be deduced like this:

<u>For the personal pronoun 'I':</u>

First person singular – I

First person plural – we

First person possessive singular – my, mine

First person possessive plural – our, ours

<u>For the personal pronoun 'you':</u>

Second person singular – you

Second person plural – you

Second person possessive singular – your

Second person possessive plural – your

<u>For the personal pronoun 'he/she/it':</u>

Third person singular – he/she/it

Third person plural – they

Third person possessive singular – his/her/its

Third person possessive plural – their/theirs

Are you thinking that it is the end of pronouns? Sorry, there is some more we need to discuss about these. Brace yourself to know.

According to the usage and type, pronouns are categorized into the following:

<u>Personal pronouns</u>

We have discussed about these in the above with elaborative examples. *I, you, he, she, it, we, they, who* are personal pronouns. It is not strictly barred, but personal pronouns mostly represent living beings.

(i) He is a great man.

(ii) She never cooks in her home

(iii) The tree has fallen across the road and it blocked all the vehicles came in that way.

(iv) The metal is shining yellow and for a moment I thought it was gold.

In the above examples, 'he' and 'she' are personal pronouns. In the sentences (iii) and (iv) 'it' the pronoun represented the inanimate things 'the tree' and 'the metal'.

The following are the examples for the usage of *'it'* as a personal pronoun

The baby is crying for *its* mother.

The horse has broken *its* leg.

The monkey lost *its* grip on the branch

'It' is used as a personal pronoun for babies and animals.

<u>Demonstrative pronouns:</u>

These pronouns demonstrate or indicate as the name suggests. That means they make us knowledgeable or let us know something. Luckily there are not many demonstrative pronouns. Just the following are having the privilege to be called as demonstrative pronouns.

This, that, these and those.

This pen on this table is good. That pen in the cupboard is bad.

'this pen' here the pen on this table.

'This' is used for the things nearby

'that pen' the pen is not here but in the cupboard some faraway.

'That' is used for the things at a distance.

These mangoes we are eating now are good. Those mangoes we ate yesterday were not tasted well. We have to see how those mangoes we eat tomorrow would be.

'These' pronoun is used for the present tense or to the things nearby.

'Those' pronoun is used for the past or future tense or to the things at a distance.

Interrogative pronouns:

Lucky you are! These pronouns are also not many, just few, **who, which, what** and **where**.

I know you are curious to know what the interrogative pronouns do or you might have guessed it by now. Interrogative pronouns are used to ask questions. Interrogative pronouns are inquisitive and knowledge thirsty.

Who asked you to do this?

Which pen you used to write the yesterday's exam?

What colour of dress I have to wear to attend that celebration?

Where we are all going?

Are you clear now? But don't come to the opinion that interrogative pronouns are having no other duty except asking questions. In some situations they can be used as relative pronouns also.

This is **what** I have asked him then.

This is the book **which** I have read on that day.

That is the place from **where** we started our journey then.

He is the person **who** asked us to do that.

By this elaboration, you came to know that there is another class of pronouns 'Relative pronouns'. Yes.

Relative Pronouns:

Relative pronouns make us more knowledgeable about something or they do emphasize something. The above examples amply serve the purpose. Anyhow I do give some more examples hereunder:

The road on **which** we travelled on that day is not even.

The book *that* I have read in the class is not good.

The movie *which* I have seen yesterday is about peacocks.

In the above sentences *'which'* and *'that'* are relative pronouns. Which is used for things without life and for animals. It can be used for singular and plural nouns also.

'The road', 'the book' and 'the movie' are the 'antecedents' of the relative pronouns 'which', 'that'. Don't be confused! You are going to be known about 'antecedents' very soon.

It may be in advance but it is better that you acquaintance with some of the uses of *'that'* here.

After adjectives in the superlative degree 'that' should be used

The best thing he ever did is *that* he never took debts.

She is the best singer *that* I have come across so far.

The strongest man in the world *that* I have seen on that day.

That follows the words *'none, nothing, only, all, same and any,'*.

All mangoes *that* we bought are sour.

He is the same person *that* we saw yesterday.

None of the above *that* we know.

Nothing *that* we see now matters in future.

Only *that* our timely advice saved him from the trouble.

That comes after interrogative pronouns also

Who *that* wrote the examination best on yesterday?

What medicine *that* he has to take to be cured?

That comes after adjectives of superlative degree

She is the most beautiful actor *that* I ever have seen

Most gracious thing *that* he did at that moment.

It has to be remembered that a relative pronoun always refers to a noun in the sentence and that noun is called as the 'antecedent' of that relative pronoun.

In the above sentences 'He is the same person', 'None of the above', 'nothing' 'only 'who' and 'what' are the antecedents of 'that'

It may be appropriate that you do know the uses of the some of the relative pronouns:

<u>Who</u>

'Who' as a relative pronoun can be used for singular and plural nouns also. But its usage is restricted only to persons. It feels too much offensive if it has been used for animals and lifeless things.

He who works hard will succeed. (Here 'he' is the antecedent for 'who')

She who won in the elections as president should come before to the meeting (Here 'she' is the antecedent for 'who')

Those who cannot work hard never can get success. (Here 'those' is the antecedent for 'who')

<u>Which</u>

'Which' would have felt some envy towards 'who' as its use is restricted only to the animals and lifeless things. That means *'which'* should be used as a relative pronoun only for animals and things without life and those animals and things can either be singular or plural.

Animals which don't bite are best to keep as pets. (Here 'animals' is the antecedent for 'which')

The rock on which he was stumbled made him come out of his thoughts. (Here 'the rock' is the antecedent for 'which')

The dog which bites should be kept as far away as possible. (Here 'the dog' is the antecedent for 'which')

<u>That</u>

'**That**' would have felt happier and both '**who**' and '**which**' do feel envy to it. It is just because it can be used as a relative pronoun for persons, animals and things also. Of course, those persons, animals and things can be either singular or plural also.

He is the person that I saw yesterday. (Here 'he' is the antecedent for 'that')

Those animals that give milk should be given good food. (Here 'those animals' is the antecedent for 'that')

The papers that have been given to him are not of good quality. (Here 'the papers' is the antecedent for 'that')

Compound relative pronouns:

There are *compound relative pronouns* also. *Whoever, whosoever, whichever, whatever, whatsoever* are called as *compound relative pronouns*. The *compound relative pronouns* don't need an antecedent. These words can be used as *compound interrogative pronouns* also.

Whoever did that will be punished.

Whosoever wants that should come and take it.

Whichever way you take, it leads you there.

Whatever you said is good to hear.

Whatsoever advised by that old man is worth following.

Compound interrogative pronouns:

Whatever you said is worth doing.

Whichever way you look at, you can find the same thing.

Indefinite pronouns:

Most of the indefinite pronouns are vague and unclear. Most of them say something but they cannot specify. Don't get angry but just they are like that. Be aware! They are very large in number.

Some, any, several, all, anyone, nobody, each, both, few, either, none, one are the few. The list is exhaustive! I demonstrate what I have said with the following examples.

Several people came there, few among them knew me.

Among those, only few knew about carpentry.

Some people born only to do good things.

What

'What' is generally used to ask questions. *'What'* is used only for things or assumptions. The specialty of *what* is; it does not need an antecedent.

What purpose will be served by your doing that?

What went wrong when we did that?

Sometimes *what* can be used referring to persons also.

What type of person you are!

What can be used in making statements also.

What he said was not that much good to hear.

That is *what* really is troubling him.

Some indefinite pronouns or indefinite pronouns sometimes give good and complete sense. They specify, make the things clear and prove themselves out of the category.

Anyone who attended the yesterday's meeting can tell about that.

None in the classroom are upto the mark.

Both of them left our house after lunch.

Each of these two roads leads to the same destination.

<u>Possessive pronouns:</u>

I think we have a little discussion about these before in this book. Yes, your assumption is right. Possessive pronouns denote possession. *My, mine, our, ours, their, theirs, his, her* are possessive pronouns. Now we shall see what type of work they would do.

Examples:

This is *my* coat.

You can also say 'this coat is *mine*'.

Our house is not far from here.

I never went to *their* house.

His character is better than *her* character.

This is her pen.

You can also say 'This pen is hers'

In the above sentences '*my*', '*our*' '*their*', '*his*' and '*her*' are possessive pronouns. As these are doing a job like adjectives, they are entitled to be called as possessive adjectives also. Let adjectives feel envy, get angry for their entitlement like this, the possessive pronouns don't care.

<u>Reciprocal pronouns:</u>

These pronouns give a great message that things need to be reciprocated. So far I know there are only two reciprocal pronouns '*each other*' and '*one another*'. If you come across any more of these, let me know I add them to the list when I update this book.

They love *each other* as no one else loved at any time before.

In the pilgrimage, they helped *one another* to do it safely and comfortably.

In general usage, '*each other*' should be used when there are only two people or things and '*one another*' when there are more than two. But now a day this rule is not followed that strictly at all.

Reflexive pronouns:

By adding '*self*' to '*my*', '*your*' '*him*' '*her*' or '*it*' we get Singular Compound Personal Pronouns. By adding '*selves*' to '*our*' '*your*' or '*them*' we get Plural Compound Personal Pronouns. The Compound Personal Pronouns are used when the action turns back to the subject itself and then they are called as Reflexive Pronouns.

He did that to *himself.*

She upgraded *herself.*

You have to do it *yourself.*

It drank the milk *itself.*

They killed *themselves.*

You neglected *yourselves* while doing that work.

We blamed *ourselves.*

Emphatic Pronouns:

These Compound Personal Pronouns shall be called as Emphatic Pronouns when they give emphasis to the noun they represent.

I do it *myself.*

Anita worked *herself* very hard.

You, *yourself,* are responsible for this.

They, *themselves,* created the havoc.

Distributive Pronouns:

When the pronouns are used to indicate only one person or thing at a time, they are called as Distributive Pronouns.

In the following sentences **'Each, either and neither'** are used as distributive pronouns.

Each of the book I have been reading is entertaining.

Either of the persons I met could not give me the solution

Neither of those movies is good to see

'Either' and 'Neither' should be used to denote only two things.

The nouns which follow the Distributive Pronouns must be in singular and should be followed by a verb in singular.

<u>Exclamatory pronouns:</u>

The pronoun which is used for exclamation is called as an exclamatory pronoun.

What! This is preposterous!

Hurrah! Go ahead!

This is the last for pronouns. Don't be relaxed yet. There is a lot we need to learn and the next Parts Of Speech is 'Verb'.

Verb

It is the most important Parts of Speech and you have to respect it as much as you can. Even you do mistakes with other parts of speech there may not be much change in the meaning but if you do mistakes with 'verb' it changes a lot the meaning of the sentence. But with attention and interest it is not difficult to master this part of speech also.

Before we delve deep into the discussion of Verb, we see what exactly it is. The following examples are waiting for your reading.

She *gave a* ball to Hari.

Micheal *is thinking* very hard to solve the problem.

They *were punished* by the teacher.

The cat *is* on the table.

In the above sentences *'gave a', 'is thinking' 'were punished' 'is'* are called as verbs. If you observe these examples carefully, you know that they are conveying an action that was done in the past *'gave a'* and *'were punished'* or an action that is going on at present *'is thinking'* or some state of a thing *'is.'*

The word used as a verb conveys an action that has taken place or is taking place or going to take place in future. All the words used to indicate the state of a thing in the past, present or in the future are also called as verbs.

Ah, you came to know what a verb is. Now we shall see the other important aspects and the usage of the verbs in detail.

Basically, in a grand manner, according to the usage of the words as verbs, the tense of the verbs are decided like this.

1. Present tense

Denotes the action that is taking place at the present moment

1. Past tense

Denotes the action that has taken place in the past

1. Future tense

Denotes the action that is going to take place in future.

Again, according to the variance in the action, each tense of these three, divided into four categories.

For better understanding of the tenses, keep the following in mind.

First Person Singular – I

First Person Plural – We

Second Person Singular – You

Second Person Plural – You

Third Person Singular – He, She, It

Third Person Plural – They

Present Tense

The first tense in the present tense is Simple Present Tense because it simply conveys whatever is happening in the very present moment. But our grammar makers assigned some more duties also to it. Just go through the following.

<u>Simple Present Tense:</u>

Now we shall see exactly for what purposes the simple present tense can be used.

i) Says general truths

Moon and stars shine in the night

Gold values a lot

ii) Says every day usual activities

I drink coffee every morning.

He reads a book before going to sleep in the night

iii) In exclamatory sentences

Alas! It bursts

Hurrah! He wins

iv) If it is fixed, simple present tense can be used for the future also.

I get there at 9.00 a.m. tomorrow

She comes here by 12.00 noon tomorrow

In clauses of time and condition, which begin with *if, till, which, where*, etc., even the meaning of it implies future, Simple Present Tense shall be used. Observe the examples to let go of your confusion.

We shall wait here till he comes.

Which decision he takes I cannot say now.

If he fulfills his promise I shall give him one lakh rupees.

Where from he comes here I don't know.

To introduce quotations by great people, Simple Present Tense is used.

Mahatma Gandhi says 'Non-violence is the greatest virtue

<u>The way Simple Present Tense forms:</u>

With First Person singular and plural we use the present tense of the verb without adding '*s*' to it.

I take my book

We go into the room

With Second Person and Third Person plural also we use the present tense of the verb without adding '*s*' to it.

They go into the room

They look into my face.

You take the book.

You sit on the bed.

But when it is Third Person singular, we use the present tense of the verb adding '*s*' to it.

He goes into the room.

He looks into my face

<u>Present Continuous Tense:</u>

This tense denotes something that is going on at present and not finished yet.

He is thinking very hard to know how to solve that problem.

Neeta is writing her examination making her all concentration on that.

The horse is running very fast.

Present Continuous Tense can be used for an action even it is not happening now but started in the past and most likely happens in the future also.

Ranjan is learning English grammar.

Ranjan started learning English grammar. Even he is doing something else at present most likely he learns it in future also.

Present continuous tense can be used for something that has been decided to be done in future. It does not care the angry looks of future tense.

He is going to his wife on tomorrow.

The bus is coming this way in the evening.

We already learnt that Simple Present Tense can be used for the things we do everyday. But this tense strongly revolted to be used for persistent bad habits. Innocent present continuous tense took up that duty. It agreed to be used for present persistent bad habits which continue in spite of threats, requests, scolding and warnings.

He is always smoking in the public areas, despite the warnings by police.

She is always cooking bad, even we requested her many a time to cook good.

<u>The way present continuous tense forms:</u>

'is' is the verb for present continuous tense if the subject is Third Person Singular. By using *'is'* after the subject and before the object we can make Present Continuous Tense for the sentences having Third Person Singular Subject.

He is working very hard.

He is taking the table with him.

'are' is the verb for present continuous tense if the subject is Third Person Plural. By using *'are'* after the subject and before the object we can make Present Continuous Tense for the sentences having Third Person Plural Subject.

They are waiting for the bus.

We are proceeding towards the college.

'are' is the verb for present continuous tense if the subject is Second Person Singular or Plural. By using 'are' after the subject and before the object we can make Present Continuous Tense for the sentences having Second Person Singular or Plural Subject.

You are writing your exam.

You all are waiting for the bus.

In Present Continuous Tense **'am'** is the verb if the subject is First Person Singular and 'are' is the verb for First Person Plural. By using 'am', 'are' after the subject and before the object we can make Present Continuous Tense for the sentences having First Person Singular or Plural Subjects.

I *am* waiting for the bus

We *are* going to the college.

Present Perfect Tense:

Now we do see how the Present Perfect Tense would be used. Even before this we have to know what is Present Perfect Tense.

The main activity of the Present Perfect Tense is to indicate the actions finished just now.

I have just finished reading the book.

She has finished writing the poem.

Past tense may feel sour, but when time is not specifically mentioned present perfect tense can be used for the past actions also.

Lal has finished his graduation.

(He might have finished his graduation two years back. But as the time is not mentioned we can use present perfect tense.)

If the time is specifically mentioned, don't dare to use Present Perfect Tense. Simple Past Tense is not such a generous one to give all the chances to other tenses. When the time is made clear, you have to use Simple Past Tense.

He went to Kolkata three days back (Never dare say He has gone to Kolkata three days back, it is a wrong usage)

She completed drawing the picture yesterday.

When we give more importance to the effect than the time when it happens, we have to use present perfect tense

He has slapped me hard and my check is still paining.

I have finished my lunch and I am feeling heavy now.

The way Present Perfect Tense forms:

For First Person Singular and Plural, for the Second Person and for the Third Person Plural *'have'* immediately follows the subject.

For the third person singular *'has'* immediately follows the subject.

Examples:

I have done my duty.

We have arrived at the cinema theatre.

She has arrived ten minutes late.

He has finished reading the book.

They have gone by the time we came.

Sometimes it is the combined verb *'has been'* or *'have been'* for the Present Perfect Tense. Just because of *'been'* it is not Present Perfect Continuous Tense. Still it is Present Perfect Tense.

<u>Present Perfect Continuous Tense:</u>

This tense may feel lonely, desolated and be quite angry with the grammar makers because it has not been assigned many duties. The main function of this tense is to denote those actions which started in the past and are still continuing.

He has been working as a servant in Sohan's family for the last 15 years

Past Tense

The verbs which denote the actions took place in the past or happened for a specific period in the past or specific state of things in the past are said to be in Past Tense. This past tense further has been divided into four categories.

<u>Simple Past Tense:</u>

For the actions done or happened in the past, the Simple Past Tense would be used.

Examples:

He went to his home on Thursday

I completed reading the book yesterday

I joined in my job two years ago

Adverbs or adverb phrases of time follow the object in simple past tense. In the above examples 'Thursday', 'yesterday' are adverbs and 'two years ago' is an adverb phrase. If there are no adverb phrases you have to use Present Perfect Tense instead of Simple Past Tense. Observe the above examples without adverbs and adverb phrases of time.

He has gone to his home

I have completed reading the book

I have joined in my job

Simple Past Tense can be used for our habits in the past.

I read English books everyday in the evening in my teenage

I drank coffee while I was in Nagpur

He slept only three hours every night while he was preparing for IAS.

<u>The way Simple Past Tense forms:</u>

The past tense of the verb simply follows subject

He drank coffee

Rony mixed with the gang.

Past Continuous Tense:

Past Continuous Tense denotes the actions went on for a considerable period of time in the past.

At that time, we were preparing our lunch.

Nickerson and John were playing tennis.

Mary was preparing for her examinations.

This tense can be used for the persistent past habits also.

Stuart was always playing tennis in his teens (Of course, he is not playing now)

Rose was continually listening to the radio for songs. (Anyhow she got cured of that habit and not listening anymore now)

I am going to say an important thing herein. Observe the following examples.

I was watching a movie interestingly when he came to my home.

While he was reading the book with all the concentration, the book dropped onto the floor.

When the other action happened while one action was going on, past continuous tense has to be used for the action that was going on and simple past tense shall be used for the action that happened.

The way Past Continuous Tense forms:

For the First Person plural, for the Second Person and the Third Person plural simply *'were'* follows the subject.

We were reading a book

You were reading a book.

They were reading a book

For the First Person Singular and the Third Person Singular simply 'was' follows the subject.

I was reading a book.

He was reading a book

Past Perfect Tense:

For an action happened at a specific point of time in the past, past perfect tense is used.

I had seen him then.

She had passed her Matriculation in the year 1996

The way the past perfect tense forms:

'had' the past perfect verb one of the rigid fellow does not allow any change in it and simply follow any subject in whichever person and number it may be without any discrimination.

The verb that follows 'had' should be in third person or past participle

Past Perfect Continuous Tense:

It is one of the tenses which laments for the lack of importance. Not many duties assigned to it. It also may be quite angry with the grammar makers. Anyhow the main duty of the past perfect continuous tense is to denote some action that started at a point of time in the past and finished at a point of time in the past.

He had been reading that book for the last two months. (He stopped reading that book in the past itself at a point of time)

Ronika had been attending that college for the last three years (She stopped attending it at a point of time in the past itself.)

The way Past Perfect Continuous Tense forms:

The compound verb *'had been'* shamelessly follow all the subjects in whichever number and person they may be without any discrimination.

In past perfect continuous tense, the verb that follows *had been* should be with *-ing.*

Future Tense

This tense can be used for all the actions that take place in future, take place and continue sometime in future, come to an end in future. It also, just like present and past, divided into four categories. They are as follows:

<u>Simple Future Tense:</u>

It mainly denotes such type of actions going to happen in future which cannot be controlled at all.

Ronika will reach Nagpur by this time tomorrow. (It cannot be controlled or changed)

The climate here will become quite hot in the month of May.

This tense can be used to express our assumptions and guesses also.

I guess he will be our next prime minister. (he may or may not be)

Simple Future Tense can be used for immediate actions without preparation

I will go there and wait for you.

She will come here at any point of time.

Simple Future Tense may be quite angry as some of the duties supposed to be done by it are assigned to the phrases *'going to'* and *'about to'"*

<u>Going to:</u>

It is used for the actions likely to happen or certain while the present insinuate them so.

The balloon is overfilled with air, it is ***going to*** burst.

Hancy completed the ninth month of her pregnancy, she is ***going to*** deliver a baby.

It is used for the actions at the nick of happening.

We have to do something; the ship is *going to* sink

We just heard some sound; the balloon is *going to* burst.

<u>About to:</u>

We can use *'about to'* for the actions take place immediately.

We have to do something, the ship is *about to* sink

We just heard some sound, the balloon is *about to* burst.

"'going to' and *'about to'* must be preceded by a *be* form *'is'* or *'are'"*

<u>The way Simple Future Tense forms:</u>

As per general practice *'shall'* follow the First Person Singular and Plural and *'will'* follow all the other persons. Anyhow this rule is not strictly followed now a day.

<u>Future Continuous Tense:</u>

Broadly Future Continuous Tense can be used for the actions that take place in future and continue for a considerable period of time. But it can be used in other ways also.

We can express our assumptions or suppositions

It will be quite cool by the time we reach there.

Mary will be on the plane by this time tomorrow.

For our plan of actions, the happenings of general course of things

I will be in Mexico by next Monday.

The mangoes will be ripe just in two days.

<u>The way Future Continuous Tense forms:</u>

'will be' follows all the subjects other than first person singular and plural in whichever number, person they may be without any discrimination.

He *will be* turned twenty by next month.

She *will be* here by this time tomorrow.

They *will be* in London by next week.

You *will be* extremely happy after reaching that place.

"'shall be' follows the subjects in First Person Singular and Plural.

I *shall be* right after him when he comes here.

We *shall be* very glad after the inheritance of the property

If a verb follows *will be*, it should be in *third person* or *past participle* like turned, blamed, aged/

<u>Future Perfect Tense:</u>

This tense can be used for actions that would be completed in future.

I *shall have* written my novel by the next week.

Mary *will have* her lunch by this time tomorrow.

If a verb follows *shall have* or *will have*, it should be in *third person* or a *past participle*

<u>The way Future Perfect Tense forms:</u>

'shall have' simply follows subjects in First Person Singular and Plural.

I shall have reached my twenty fifth year by this time next year.

We shall have our lunch by this time tomorrow.

'will have' simply follows all the subjects other than First Person Singular and Plural

He will have completed his exercise after one hour or so.

You will have got your medal tomorrow morning.

They will have reached this place at any point of time.

<u>Future Perfect Continuous Tense:</u>

This tense can be used for the actions started, going on already and continue in future also.

I shall have been teaching grammar for more than twenty years by next year.

She will have been cooking in the home for ten years by next month.

<u>The way Future Perfect Continuous Tense forms:</u>

After the First Person Singular and Plural *'shall have been'* follows. All the other persons whether singular or plural *'will have been'* follows.

This tense is not very much in use now a day. So don't break your head to understand this.

So far we have discussed about basic present, past and future tenses. Now we are going to discuss threadbare about verbs.

If the verb is more than one word, like a clause, it is called a predicate.

It *is going to* rain at anytime now.

The train *is about to* leave.

In the above sentences '*is going to*' and '*is about to*' are called as predicates.

In fact verbs are two types: (i) Transitive verbs and (ii) Intransitive verbs

i. Transitive verbs

When there is an action and the action goes from the subject to the object, the verbs used for such action are called as Transitive verbs.

John *threw* the ball

Mary *received* the letter

In the above sentences '*threw*' and '*received*' arc Transitive verbs

Even most of the times Transitive Verbs take only single noun sometimes they take two nouns also. In such sentences one noun is called as direct object and other noun is called as indirect object. As such, it need not be stressed here that Dative Case is possible only with transitive verbs. (We already discussed about Dative Case). The following examples make it more clear to you.

He threw the ball to Williams.

John received the book from Mary

There are some verbs like *kick, want, throw, etc.* which cannot be used as intransitive at all. The list is exhaustive!

i. Intransitive verbs

If the action stops with the subject itself and there is no object in the sentences, the verbs in such sentences are called as Intransitive Verbs.

The sea is *roaring* like a lion

He *chuckled* in himself after hearing the news.

In the above sentences '*roaring*' and '*chuckled*' are intransitive verbs.

When the subject and object indicate the same person in a sentence, the verb usage in such sentences is called as *reflexive usage*.

He tried himself a lot to do that.

She worried herself for the situation she was in for a long time.

It is better not classify any verb as either transitive or intransitive because a transitive verb can be used as intransitive and an intransitive verb can be used as transitive. So we can better say whether a verb used as transitively or intransitively rather than fixing it transitive or intransitive.

Observe the following examples to enlighten yourself about this aspect.

I *felt* severe pain in my cut finger (*felt* Transitive)

How did she *feel* about that? (*feel* Intransitive)

There are some verbs that cannot be used as Transitive Verbs at all. They are the verbs like *laugh, smile, occur*, etc. The list is exhaustive!

Even most of the Intransitive verbs are so generous and liberal that they don't want any word, some intransitive verbs demand a word beside them to give complete sense. Enjoy the following examples.

He *seems angry.*

John *became class leader.*

Mary *appears non-chalant.*

Such types of Intransitive verbs which demand a word beside them to give complete meaning are called as *verbs of incomplete predication.*

In the above examples '*seems*', '*became*' and '*appears*' are called as *verbs of incomplete predication.*

Such words which satisfy the thirst of verbs of incomplete predication are called as *complement of the verb* or *completion of the predicate*.

In the above examples '*angry*', '*class leader*' and '*non-chalant*' are *complement of the verb* or *completion of the predicate*

The word which satisfies the desire of an intransitive verb to give complete sense can be a noun or an adjective. If it is a noun it is called as *predicative noun* or if it is an adjective it is called as *predicative adjective*.

Observe the following examples:

We made him *the leader*

That black thing on the table is *a dog*

In the above sentences '*the leader*' and the '*a dog*' are predicative nouns.

The building appears *beautiful.*

Her smile looks *gorgeous*.

In the above sentences '*beautiful*' and the '*gorgeous*' are predicative adjectives.

Sometimes the predicative complement describes the subject. In such situations it is called as *Subjective Complement*. The following examples make it clear to you.

Rony is a *tall person*

Jasmine is a *beautiful girl*

In the above examples '*tall person*' and '*beautiful girl*' are subjective complements. The subjective complement must be in the same case of the subject i.e. nominative case.

Not just the subjects, sometimes objects also crave for a complement to give full meaning. Observe the following examples.

In the year 1996 they elected Williams *as Chairman*

By telling jokes continuously, Rony made the girl *joyous*

In the above examples '*as Chairman*' and '*joyous*' are *objective complements.*

Verbs do have *present tense, past tense* and *past participle*.

Speak (present tense)

Spoke (past tense)

Spoken (past participle)

Tell (present tense)

Told (past tense)

Told (past participle)

There are innumerable ways to present tense verbs to transform into past tense and past participle. By adding -ing to the present tense verb, the continuous tense verb to the three tenses, present participle and gerund are formed.

In the Simple Present Tense, if the subject is in First Person singular or plural, or in Second person or third person plural the same verb *speak* should be used.

I speak.

We speak

You speak

They speak

In the Simple Present Tense, if the subject is in third person singular the verb *speaks* should be used. 's' needs to be added to the verb

He *speaks.*

She *speaks.*

The verb *speak* shall be changed into spoke, spoken, speaking according to the tense other than Simple Present Tense. For most of the verbs, the same principle can be applied safely.

Just like the subjects Verbs also do have singular and plural

Speaks (singular) speak (plural)

Laughs (singular) laugh (plural)

Tries (singular) try (plural)

The most common usage to make plural verb to singular is to add '*s*' to it. It is important to keep in mind that '*s*' to the singular verb should be added only when the sentence is in simple present.

If the subject is in singular the verb also must be singular.

Nikhil speaks English beautifully.

Rose sings very nice.

If the subject is in plural the verb also must be in plural.

They *speak* only French.

I think that they *try* it again.

By the above it can be neatly deduced that the Verb must agree with the person and number of the Subject

Verbs can further be classified into two categories:

(i) Regular Verbs

(ii) Irregular Verbs

Regular Verbs form their *past* and *past participle* simply by adding *–ed* to the present. Observe the following examples:

Walk (present)

Walked (past)

Walked (past participle)

But Irregular Verbs can form their *past* and *past participle* by many ways

Sometimes the *same present tense* verb is used for *past* and *past participle* also

Put (present)

Put (past)

Put (past participle)

Hit (present)

Hit (past)

Hit (past participle)

Read (present)

Read (past)

Read (past participle)

Even there is no change in the word *read* for the three tenses, while pronouncing the *past* and *past participles, read* should be pronounced as *red*.

For some verbs *past* and *past participles* remain the same while the *present* is a different word

Win (present)

Won (past)

Won (past participle)

Dig (present)

Dug (past)

Dug (past participle)

Sit (Present)

Sat (past)

Sat (past participle)

Build (present)

Built (past)

Built (past participle)

For some irregular verbs different words would be used for the three *present, past* and *past participle.*

Drink (present)

Drank (past)

Drunk (past participle)

Get (present)

Got (past)

Gotten (past participle)

Some verbs do have regular and irregular formation also.

Smell – Regular Verb

Smell (present)

Smelled (past)

Smelled (past participle)

Smell – Irregular Verb

Smell (present)

Smelt (past)
Smelt (past participle)
Leap – Regular Verb
Leap (present)
Leaped (past)
Leaped (past participle)
Leap – Irregular Verb
Leap (present)
Leapt (past)
Leapt (past participle)
<u>**Raise and rise:**</u>
The meaning of both these words is the same– make something up or something going up. But there are other differences between these words.
<u>**Raise**</u>
Raise is a Regular Verb
Raise (present)
Raised (past)
Raised (past participle)
Raise is a Transitive Verb. It takes an object.
John *raised* the rice bag from the floor and put it on the table.
She *raised* her voice to be heard in the whole hall
<u>**Rise**</u>
Rise is an Irregular Verb
Rise (present)
Rose (past)
Rose (past participle)
Rise is an Intransitive Verb. It must not followed by an object.
The air *rises* steadily upwards.
The balloon *rose* into the air.
She *rose* from the chair she sat
<u>**Hang**</u>

Hang is an Irregular and Transitive Verb. Observe the three tenses of it.

Hang (present)

Hung (past)

Hung (past participle)

Hang is generally used in the meaning that something supported by a rope or hooked onto a rope or something else in the air after linking upto something or something came down or drooped down from the air.

He *hung* his shirt to the door hook.

She *hung* her head in shame.

But there is another past participle for *hang* that is *hanged*. This hanged is used for only one thing and nothing else. That is when someone is killed by a rope or when someone is suspended by a rope to cause his death.

The dacoit was *hanged* in his thirtieth year itself for the heinous crimes he committed.

They observed him with pity while he was *hanged* by a rope.

It may be appropriate to you to know about *'phrase'* and *'clause.'*

Phrase:

A group of words can be called as *phrase*. They do give meaning but not complete meaning. They don't have subject and verb.

She prepared to go out *in the evening*.

It is raining here *from the morning* itself.

Clause:

Clause also is a group of words. Sometimes it just becomes a part of a sentence and does not give complete meaning. Then it is called as dependent clause. Sometimes it gives complete meaning. Then it is called as independent clause. Whether it is dependent or independent, clause does have an independent subject and verb.

Dependent clause examples:

He feels angry

He draws picture

When he came

Then she went out

Independent clause examples:

She sat on the mat.

The dog ran quickly from there.

The Infinitive

Sometimes verbs preceded by *'to'* are used like nouns. These nouns can be used as subjects and objects also. It almost does the work of noun as such called as *Verbal Noun*.

Examples:

'to make', 'to go', 'to sing', 'to love' and 'to sit'

To make chocolates is not easy

He is ready *to go* anywhere

That is the only place to us *to go.*

In the above examples *'to make'* and *'to go'* are infinitives.

The Participle

By taking *–ing* with them verbs can be used like adjectives. These are verbal adjectives and called as *participle*.

Hearing, singing, flying, playing, roaring.

Hearing the song, he felt so much joyous.

Playing nice, he won in the game.

Participles which are formed by adding –ing to the present tense verb are called as *Present Participles*.

Maddened by anger, he hit the wall with his hand.

Sodden with water, he could not travel far.

The above words '*Maddened*' and '*Sodden*' are called as past participles. This is in fact the third form of the verb and denotes a completed action.

Usually, the present participle, gives active in meaning whereas the past participle gives passive in meaning. You can understand this better after you learn Active Voice and Passive Voice. Anyhow, observe the following examples:

The spent money – the money that is spent

The wasted energy – the energy that is wasted

The roaring lion – the lion that is roaring

The changing circumstances – circumstances that are changing

Participles either present or past must be attached to a subject, otherwise the usage becomes incorrect.

Hearing his voice like that, I suspected he was drunk.

Trained a dog in such a way is indeed a difficult thing.

The Gerund

Just like the present participles, the gerunds also are formed by adding –ing to the present tense verbs.

Hearing, singing, flying, playing, roaring.

But what is the difference between a present participle and gerund? Just pay intention and you can easily understand.

The ***present participle*** is a verbal adjective and it does the work of an adjective. It must be attached to a noun.

Hearing the sound, I understood the bomb was blasted.

Trying his hard, he succeeded in the exam.

The ***gerund*** is a verbal noun and it does the work of a noun. It need not be followed or preceded by a noun. As gerund is a 'verbal noun' it does almost all the duties of a noun.

Hearing is one of the senses we have.

We went to that place after ***hearing*** the sound.

Changing according to the circumstances is a great and useful quality.

In this environment we need ***changing*** of clothes.

Active Voice and Passive Voice

This is one aspect that you need to pay more interest to understand. In active voice it is shown that subject does something to the object. Observe the following:

Williams *kicked* the ball

Stuart *told* the story to the children

In the above examples the verbs '*kicked*' and '*told*' are said to be in Active Voice.

In passive voice it is shown as something has been done to the subject. Object in the active voice becomes the subject in passive voice.

Observe the following examples.

The ball *was kicked* by Williams

The story *was told* by Stuart to the children.

In the above examples the verbs '*was kicked*' and '*was told*' are said to be in Passive Voice.

In Active Voice and Passive Voice also Verbs play the main role. One important thing here is: only transitive verbs can play the role of passive voice as they have an object. Since the intransitive verbs don't have an object, however much they crave, they cannot become passive.

The way active voice verbs transform into passive voice

For the simple past tense:

Nikhil told the story (Active voice)

The story was told by Nikhil. (Passive Voice)

Ranjan made the candles (Active Voice)

The candles were made by Ranjan. (Passive voice)

You have to simply place *'was'* or *'were'* before the main verb according to the subject (which is object in active voice) person and number to transform Simple Past Tense sentences from active into passive.

<u>For the past continuous tense:</u>
They were changing their clothes. (Active Voice)
The clothes were being changed by them. (Passive Voice)
He was reading the book. (Active Voice)
The book was being read by him (Passive Voice)
He was taking mangoes with him (Active Voice)
The mangoes were being taken by him (Passive Voice)

You have to simply place *'being'* after *'was'* or *'were'* and the verb *'was'* would be changed into *'were'* if the subject in passive voice is plural to transform Past Continuous Tense sentences from Active into Passive.

<u>For the past perfect tense:</u>
She had learned the music lesson (Active Voice)
The music lesson had been learnt by her (Passive Voice)
She had taken the mangoes with her (Active Voice)
The mangoes had been taken by her (Passive Voice)

You have to simply place *'been'* after *'had'* to transform Past Perfect Tense sentences from active into passive. Sometimes, *with* in active voice shall be changed into *by* in passive voice.

Past perfect continuous tense may frustrate a lot because it cannot transform into passive. Means, there is no passive voice to Past Perfect Continuous Tense.

<u>For simple present tense:</u>
He brings the ball into his hands (Active voice)
The ball is brought by him into his hands. (Passive Voice)
He brings the flowers into his hands (Active voice)
The flowers are brought by him into his hands. (Passive voice)
The elephant brings me with its trunk (Active voice)

I am brought by the elephant by its trunk. (Passive voice)

You have to simply place '*am, is, are*' before '*verb*' according to the subject (which is object in active voice) person and number to transform Simple Present Tense sentences from active into passive.

<u>For present continuous tense:</u>

They are dragging the elephant with them. (Active voice)

The elephant is being dragged by them. (Passive voice)

They are dragging the monkeys with them. (Active voice)

The monkeys are being dragged by them (Passive voice)

They are dragging me with them (Active voice)

I am being dragged by them. (Passive voice)

They are dragging you (Active voice)

You are being dragged by them. (Passive voice)

You have to simply place '*is being*' or '*am being*' or '*are being*' before '*verb*' according to the subject (which is object in active voice) person and number to transform Present Continuous Tense sentences from Active into Passive. The '*verb*' also changes into past participle. Some additional minor changes also have to be made. In the passive voice sentences in the above examples '*by*' replaced the word '*with*.'

Past perfect continuous tense also has to feel lot of frustration. Because it also does not have passive voice.

<u>Simple Future Tense:</u>

In the future tense, only Simple Future Tense and Future Perfect Tense have the privilege to transform themselves into passive. It may be quite frustrating to the remaining tenses in future but they are helpless.

I will buy mangoes. (Active Voice)

Mangoes will be bought by me. (Passive Voice)

They will buy mangoes (Active Voice)

Mangoes will be bought by them. (Passive Voice)

We shall buy the tickets (Active Voice)

The tickets shall be bought by them (Passive Voice)

You have to simply place **'be'** after **'will'** or **'shall'** to transform the Simple Future Tense sentences from active into passive.

<u>Future Perfect Tense:</u>

I shall have my lunch by then

Lunch shall have been by me by then

They will have their lunch by then.

Lunch will have been by them by then.

You have to simply place **'been'** after **'will have'** or **'shall have'** to transform the Future Perfect Tense sentences from active into passive.

In all the tenses, the **'verb'** transforms into past participle in Passive Voice Sentences.

Now we shall see how to change active voice into passive voice if the sentences are in dative case.

Nath gave a book to John

A book was given to John.

John was given a book by Nath.

Lata threw the ball to Vamsi

The ball was thrown to Vamsi by Lata

Vamsi was thrown the ball by Lata

Chitra broke the window with a stone

The window was broken by Chita with a stone

The window was broken with a stone by Chitra

Adjective

The adjective is a noun qualifier. It adds something to noun. Observe the following examples.

Ratan is a *clever* boy

There are *five* bananas on the table.

After all their lunch, *some* curd was left in the pot

This road sure leads you to correct destination.

In the above examples '*clever*', '*five*', '*some*' and '*this*' are adjectives.

The adjectives are usually placed before the noun they are qualifying. This type of usage is called as ***Attributive Usage.*** Observe the following examples.

Nikhil is a *good* boy.

Mary is a *clever* girl.

In the above examples '*good*' and '*clever*' adjectives are used *attributively.*

Sometimes adjectives used along with the predicate or verb and form part of it. This type of usage called as ***Predicative Usage.***

Mary is *clever.*

The sky is *blue*

In the above examples '*clever*' and '*blue*' adjectives are used *Predicatively.*

According to their usage adjectives are divided into following categories:

Adjectives of Quality:

These adjectives tell us about the type and quality of a noun

Nikhil is a *clever* boy.

She is an ***industrious*** girl.

In the above examples, '***clever***' and '***industrious***' are adjectives of quality.

The Adjectives of Quality are also called as Descriptive Adjectives.

<u>Proper Adjectives:</u>

The adjectives formed from proper nouns are called as Proper Adjectives

The following are the examples

American novels, Singapore biscuits.

<u>Adjectives of Quantity:</u>

The adjectives which tell us about the quantity of noun are called as Adjectives of Quantity.

She is ***little*** intelligent

Few people do have patience.

Much was said about that topic then.

At that time the voltage is ***very high***

In the above examples the words '***little***', '***few***', '***much***' and '***very high***' are Adjectives of Quantity.

<u>Adjectives of Number:</u>

These adjectives tell us about the number.

There are ***five*** pens on the table.

Four chairs are placed in that room.

In the above examples '***five***' and '***Four***' are Adjectives of Number.

The other name for Adjectives of Number is Numerical Adjectives.

These Adjectives of Number can be further divided into three categories.

<u>(1) Definite Numerical Adjectives:</u>

These adjectives tell us the exact and definite number.

One mango, four girls, three boys, etc.

These Definite Numerical Adjectives can be further divided into two categories:

<u>Cardinals:</u>

One, two, three..........

When we have to say how many we do use cardinals

One boy came here.

Two mangoes fallen from the tree

Three thieves ran in this way.

In the above examples '*one*', '*two*' and '*three*' are cardinal adjectives.

<u>Ordinals:</u>

First, Second, Third..........

When we do say order we have to use ordinals.

The *second* chapter in this book is very good.

He is the *first* man came to our house.

The *third* mango is quite sour.

In the above examples '*second*', '*first*' and '*third*' are ordinal adjectives.

(ii) Indefinite Numeral Adjectives:

These adjectives are quite irreverent and they don't tell us exact number.

Some men are lazy

Few mangoes are left to the tree

I received *several* letters on this day.

In the above examples '*Some*', '*Few*' and '*several*' are Indefinite Numeral Adjectives.

(iii) <u>Distributive Numeral Adjectives:</u>

These adjectives tell about each and everything.

Each of these mangoes is sour.

Each person in that team is honest and trustworthy.

Every person here knows about it.

*Every*thing here was paints in red.

In the above examples '*each*' and '*every*' are *distributive numeral adjectives*. Only each and every can be used as *distributive numeral adjectives.*

Distributive adjectives precede the noun and the verb in those sentences must be in singular.

Demonstrative Adjectives:

These adjectives show or indicate something in particular.

This guava among those is particularly sour.

This boy got first rank in his class.

That person is not honest.

That woman talks very loud.

Those people are not very rich

Such means are foul.

In the above examples '*this*' '*that*', '*those*' and '*such*' are *Demonstrative Adjectives*.

Interrogative Adjectives:

These adjectives are used to ask the questions.

In *what* bus you do get to go to your college?

Which shirt you are going to wear?

In *which* college she is studying?

In the above examples '*what*' and '*which*' are *Interrogative Adjectives*.

Emphasizing Adjectives:

The adjectives which are used to emphasize the nouns are called as Emphasizing Adjectives.

I have my *own* car.

She saw it with her *own* eyes.

That *very* pen she bought yesterday.

In the above examples '*own*' and '*very*' are *Emphasizing Adjectives*.

Exclamatory Adjectives:

Most usually only '*what*' '*how*' can be used as exclamatory adjectives. They are used to express something surprising in noun.

What a big snake!

What a nice picture!

How nice that show is!

That and This:

That and this may feel so happy because these are the only adjectives which change according to the number of the noun.

That book (singular)

Those books (plural)

This book (singular)

These books (plural)

The way adjectives form:

Nouns contribute a lot in formation of adjectives.

Woman – womanly

Man – manly

Child – childish

Some adjectives come from verbs also:

Talk – talkative

Move – movable

Comparison of Adjectives

The most important aspect in the adjectives is comparison. Adjectives sometimes tell the quality of the nouns.

There are three categories in Comparison of Adjectives:

<u>Positive Degree:</u>

In positive degree the adjectives simply tell the existence of some quality in a noun.

This mango is *sweet*

That book is *good* to read.

These are *fine* clothes.

In the above examples '*sweet*', '*good*' and '*fine*' adjectives are in positive degree.

<u>Comparative Degree:</u>

Comparative degree can be used when we compare two things with one another just like in the following examples.

John is *taller than* Williams.

This pen writes *better than* that pen.

In the above examples '*taller*' and '*better*' are in Comparative Degree. In comparative degree usually *than* is used.

<u>Superlative Degree:</u>

The usage of Superlative Degree comes into play when we compare more than two things or when we say the highest quality in something.

a. This mango is the *best* among all those.
b. He is the *richest* person in that town.
c. The *best* idea!

d. The *richest* woman!

In the above examples **best** and **richest** are in Superlative Degree. In (a) and (b) sentences they are used in comparison. In (c) and (d) sentences they are just indicating the highest quality.

Now we shall see how the comparative and superlative degrees form. Most often they take their form from the positive degree itself

Tall (positive)

Taller (Comparative)

Tallest (Superlative)

By adding *-er* to the positive - comparative degree and by adding *-est* to the positive - superlative degree form in most cases.

Charming (positive)

More charming (comparative)

Most charming (Superlative)

Handsome (positive)

More handsome (comparative)

Most handsome (Superlative)

For many more adjectives, by placing **more** before the positive - comparative degrec and by placing **most** before the positive - superlative degree, form

When we compare two qualities in the same person or thing we should not use –er degree. We have to say it like this.

Sugar is more **tasty** than healthy

He is more **clever** than brave.

In the above examples if you use **–er** with **tasty** and **clever** they become wrong.

Remember, when you compare things in the following manner, the former must be excluded from the latter

Rice is the best crop than any **other** crop.

Television is more entertaining than any **other** entertainment.

If you don't use *other* in the above examples, the sentences become wrong.

<u>Later, latest:</u>
Whenever we refer *time* we use *later* and *latest*
Howrah train comes *later*.
The *latest* political news is this.

<u>Latter, last:</u>
Whenever we refer *position* we use *latter* and *last*
The *latter* part of this bridge is dilapidated.
The *last* person in that queue is angry.

<u>Elder, eldest:</u>
Elder and *eldest* are used only for family members. These adjectives are deprived the authority to be used with things and other persons.

Elder is used when there are only two family members
Stuart is *elder* to Smith
Mary is *elder* to Jasmine
Than sure feels quite angry here. It is banned from following *elder*. Only the preposition *'to'* should follow *elder.*

Eldest should be used where there are more than two.
He is the *eldest* in his family

<u>Older, oldest:</u>
Older and *oldest* should be quite happy because they can be used for all persons and things including family members. Here *elder, eldest* may feel grudge but these adjectives don't care. Grammar makers don't want to make *'than'* to frustrate here. So it is allowed to follow *older*. You can safely say *'older than'*.

Older is used when there are only two things to compare.
I am *older than* my sister.
This building is *older than* that bridge.
Oldest is used when there are more than two things to compare.
It is the *oldest* building in this town.
He is the *oldest* person in his family.

Farther:

Farther is used to denote distance.

Railway station is *farther* from here than bus station.

Police station is two kilometers *farther* from here.

Further:

Further is used to denote additional.

There are no *further* pictures in this book.

There are no *further* insults to him after that.

Certain words lost their comparative capacity (I don't know where and when) and they have to be used only as positives. The following are those poor ones.

Utter, Former, elder, latter, outer, inner, upper.

Once again quite an insult to *than.* It is banned to follow these words also. That means you should not use *than* after these words.

It is *utter* surprise to us!

The *former* teacher is more knowledgeable.

Than is insulted more than once in fact. It is strictly banned to follow some words ending in *–or.* The following are the examples of those words.

Anterior, posterior, superior, prior, senior, junior, interior.

He is *junior* to his roommates in the college.

She is *senior* to him and more experienced in her profession.

Adjectives expressing qualities must not be compared.

Perfect, eternal, round, square, universal, unique, etc. words must not be compared.

For example,

You cannot be more perfect. You can be perfect.

Literary works of Mary cannot be more unique, they are unique.

Sometimes adjectives can be used like nouns. We have to place 'the' article before them then.

As plural nouns:

The rich (rich people) can enjoy whatever they want.

The poor (poor people) deprived of many enjoyments that the rich (rich people) can enjoy.

The literate (educated people) can have more advantages than the illiterate (uneducated people)

<u>As singular nouns:</u>

If you go into the garden, you can see ***the beauty*** of it.

If you see and talk with her, you can understand ***the elegancy*** in her.

You know, despite the sour feeling of adjectives, nouns also are given a chance to be used as adjectives sometimes. The following examples amply make it clear to you.

He is working as a ***room*** boy.

She is the ***door*** person there.

Proper nouns also sometimes can be used as adjectives.

Indian movies

American literature.

All proper nouns cannot jump themselves with joy to be used as adjectives. Some proper nouns can be used as adjectives and most of them have to allow some change in them to be used as adjectives. Just observe the above examples India became Indian and America became American.

But some proper nouns have the facility to be used as adjectives without any change in them.

Singapore biscuits

The Articles

The other most important aspect in adjectives after comparison is the Articles. Feel happy, the articles are not many, they are just three, *a, an* and ***the***.

These articles can further be divided into two: Indefinite Articles and Definite Article.

<u>Indefinite Articles:</u>

'*A*' and '*an*' are called as Indefinite Articles because they don't specify things.

'*A*' boy came here.

Last Thursday '*a*' mongoose came into our house.

'*An*' should be used in the place of '*a*' when the beginning letter of the noun is any of ***a,e,i,o or u***

An apple, an arrow, an additional chapter.

When it sounds like '*yu*' even the noun begins with the letter '*u*' the article '*a*' only should be used.

a union, a university,

Similarly, when it sounds like '*w*' even the noun begins with the letter '*o*' the article '*a*' only should be used.

a one-ink pot, a one-time opportunity.

But when the beginning of the noun sounds like an vowel, even it starts with letter '**h**', '**an**' can be used.

an hour, an hotel, an historical place, an heir

<u>Definite Article:</u>

'the' is the Definite Article because it specifies, denotes and indicates something without any fear.

It is *the* table we bought on that day.

He is *the* person met me on yesterday.

'the' can be used with superlative degree when we say the highest quality in something.

He is *the best* in his class.

She is *the glamour* queen.

With Ordinal Numeral Adjectives, *'the'* can be used.

the first chapter, the third drink, the tenth man

When we do use an adjective, without noun

The rich, the poor, the honest,

<u>The instances when articles should not be used:</u>

Before substances and abstract nouns when they are used in general sense. In other words, articles should not be used before uncountable nous.

Silver is not as precious as gold.

But you can use articles before uncountable nouns also when you specify

The *silver* used for making this pot is two kilograms.

I have got a *silver* medal.

The *kindness* in him is great

A kind-hearted person

When we use plural countable nouns in general sense, we must not use *'the'*

Women are courageous

Men make sometimes mistakes

I like ripe mangoes

When we say in general sense we should not use *'the'* before *breakfast*, *lunch* and *dinner*.

I have my *breakfast* at usual time.

We will have our *lunch* in the hotel on this day.

Yesterday they have their *dinner* in the home itself.

But when we want to make it particular, we have to use *'the'*.

I cannot have the *breakfast* at the usual time on this day.

The dinner we have taken at our sister's home yesterday was very nice.

The lunch we are going to take on this day is very special

Before languages also we should not use *'the'*.

I learnt *Tamil* in Madras

She does not know how to speak *English*

We should not use *'the'* with nouns like hospital, church, school, playground, temple, university when we go to these places for their usual purpose.

As he became seriously ill, he was taken to *hospital*.

She returned from *college* at 8.00 p.m.

He went to *playground* to play football.

We play hockey in *playground*.

When these places are mentioned for other than their primary purposes, *'the'* can be used.

He went to '*the hospital*' to meet his friend there.

Nikhil went to '*the university*' to collect donations for his cause.

We should not use *'the'* before uncle, father, mother, sister, etc. relations.

Yesterday *our uncle* came to our home.

Nikhil's *father* is a professor and *mother* is a house wife.

Adverb

dverb is another Parts of Speech waiting all this time for the pleasure of being learnt by you. Before plunge ourselves deep into that, it is important to have a brief idea about it.

An adverb is a word that modifies a verb, an adjective or another adverb

(i) The deer was *eating* the leaves *slowly*

(ii) She wore a '**big**' '**red**' colour sari.

(iii) The lion is running '*quickly*' '*without looking back*'.

In sentence (i) the adverb *slowly* modifying the verb *eating*

In sentence (ii) the adverb *big* modifying the adjective *red*

In sentence (iii) the adverb *without looking back* modifying another adverb *quickly*

<u>According to their usage, the adverbs are divided into following categories:</u>

<u>Adverbs of time:</u>

These adverbs denote a particular time.

I heard the news *yesterday.*

She arrives here *tomorrow.*

The event will take place only in the *next year*.

In the above examples '*yesterday*', '*tomorrow*' and '*next year*' are adverbs of time.

<u>Adverbs of Frequency:</u>

These adverbs tell us the number, how many times.

She saw him *two* times on that day.

Rose ran the needle into her hand *three* times.

Stuart went after the donkey *four* times.

In the above examples '*two*' '*three*' and '*four*' are adverbs of frequency.

Usually adverbs of frequency are put between the subject and the verb if the verb consists only one word, first word of the verb if the verb consists more than one word or after the object if there is an object.

I *once in a week* have my lunch at hotel.

She has *never* seen a person like him before.

John went after the monkey *five* times.

Adverbs of frequency placed after the verb, if the verb consists any of *am, is, was or were*

I am never interested in movies.

He is always neglecting his studies.

She was always preparing food at home.

We were quickly changed our places.

Adverbs of place:

These adverbs denote the place.

She went *there* only to inquire about him.

Williams comes *here* at any moment of time.

In the above examples '*there*' and '*here*' are adverbs of place.

Adverbs of Place should be placed after the verb.

In the above examples '*there' and 'here*' are placed after the verb.

Adverbs of manner:

These adverbs denote how a thing has been done

Nikhil read the letter *slowly and clearly*.

She went there *quickly*.

Rose is walking *slowly*.

In the above examples '*slowly and clearly*' and '*quickly*' are adverbs of manner.

Adverbs of manner should be placed after the verb or if there is an object in the sentence it should be placed after the object.

In the above examples '***slowly and clearly***' and '***quickly***' are placed after the object and ***slowly*** placed after the verb.

Adverbs of Degree:

These adverbs denote the degree, what extent. These adverbs are also called as Adverbs of Quantity.

He ran only ***half mile*** in the race.

Rose drank ***full milk*** in the glass.

In the above examples '***half mile***' and '***full milk***' are adverbs of quantity.

Adverbs of Affirmation and Negation

These adverbs simply affirm or negate just as the name suggests.

I ***do*** solve this problem now itself. (Adverb of Affirmation)

Sirisha ***did not*** see him for a long time. (Adverb of Negation)

Adverbs of Reason

These adverbs tell us about the reason.

He could not contradict with me on that issue, '***therefore***', he has to agree.

She did not do the homework, '***hence***', received the punishment.

Nikhil's willpower is great, '***so***' he could remain calm bearing the pain.

In the above examples '***therefore***', '***hence***', and '**so**' are Adverbs of Reason.

Adverbs of Interrogation

How she is walking on the road?

Where she went last night?

Why she is talking in such a way?

In the above examples '***how***', '***where***', and '**why**' are Adverbs of Interrogation.

The most important thing here is, you can say whether a word is an adjective or adverb, only by the usage of it in a sentence. Just by looking at a word you cannot say whether it is an adjective or an adverb or what type of adverb it is.

Words related to weight, measurement, time, place, distance, degree, value, etc. even they are nouns, sometimes used as adverbs. These adverbs are called as *adverbial accusatives*.

His fever lasted *a week.*

Rose ran *a mile* to complete the race.

The pole is *two feet high*

In the above examples '*a week*', '*a mile*', and '*two feet high*' are *adverbial accusatives*.

Adjectives cannot feel monopolistic, proud and haughty thinking that only they are having the capacity of comparison. Adverbs also have the capacity of comparison and they also are used to compare.

Adjectives may get once again angry because the rules for formation of adverbs are also just like the rules of formation of adjectives.

By adding *–er* to the positive - comparative adverb forms and by adding *–est* to the positive - superlative adverb forms.

Long (positive)

Longer (comparative)

Longest (superlative)

Soon (positive)

Sooner (comparative)

Soonest (superlative)

By adding *–more* to the positive - comparative adverbs form and by adding *–most* to the positive, superlative adverbs form - if the words are ending in *-ly*.

Skillfully (positive)

More skillfully (comparative)

Most skillfully (superlative)

But there is an exception to the adverb *early*

Early (positive)

Earlier (comparative)

Earliest (superlative)

Adverbs cannot feel too proud like adjectives because their comparison capacity is quite limited. Only the adverbs of *manner, degree* and *time* can have the comparison.

As adverbs are feeling frustrated as they are placed every time either after the verb or after the object if there is one, '*have to*' and '*used to*' became generous and agreed to the placement of the adverb before them. As such you have to place the adverb before *have to* and *used to* in a sentence.

You *rather have to* take cash instead of cheque.

I *never used to* blame others.

<u>Enough:</u>

Remember, the adverb *enough* has to be put always after the word it qualifies

Do we have rice *enough* in our house?

Nikhil has money *enough* to buy the car.

But this rule is disregarded in general usage.

<u>Only:</u>

The adverb '*only*' should be placed before the word it qualifies.

He has *only* one pen to write the examination.

There is *only* one way to go there.

You have to *only* ask

Adverbs of time *always, never, ever, often, seldom, sometimes, frequently, usually, etc.* also should be placed before the verbs they modify. These also would have been fought with the grammar makers and got the chance to be placed before the verb,

She *always* goes to the market in the evening.

That dog *never* does bark at the people it knows

He *ever* went to their home empty handed (That means he never went to their home empty handed)

She *often* leaves the home unlocked.

That dog *seldom* barks at day time.

We *sometimes* feel lonely.

He *frequently* visited Thomas' home in those days.

She *usually* distributes sweets to neighbors on festival days.

If we have to use an adverb with the verb –to be, that must be put after the verb.

(Am, is, was, were, be, being, been -—are called as verbs of –to be)

She *is always* on time to school.

He *was never* attended the office in time in those days.

We *were never* scolded by our parents

In case the verb consists more than one word, the adverbs of time should be placed after the first word of the verb.

She has *just* finished her work

They have *almost* been ready for the meeting.

By the time they go home, Chandra has *already* been there.

You may better understand the usage of some adverbs.

Very

'Very' should be used with the adverbs and adjectives in positive degree.

She is *very* fast in doing her work

He was *very* happy then as he passed his exams in first rank.

'Very' should be used with present participles

What he said is *very entertaining*!

It is *very amusing* to look at her so.

Much

'Much' should be used with the adverbs and adjectives in comparative degree.

She is *much* earlier to the office than before.

Nath did it *much* better than Mukund

Today is *much* hotter than yesterday

'*Much*' should be used with past participles

He is a *much talented* person!

I was *much alarmed* on hearing that.

But ***very much*** also is common in usage and I don't know whether the usage of it like that is agreed by the grammar makers or not.

I am ***very much*** happy to hear it so.

Lata was ***very much*** pleased when she heard that her sister's marriage was settled with Muchikund.

<u>Too</u>

Sometimes *'too'* is used in the place of *'very'.* Of course, *'very'* may not get angry to give its place to *'too'* but it is not the approved usage by grammar makers. Moreover *'too'* has a friend *'to'* and most of the times where *'too'* is used *'to'* also should be used after it. The exact meaning of 'too' is unnecessarily excessive, unbearably more, more than expected or need to be.

It is ***too*** hot ***to*** drink.

Too much of water has been poured ***to*** extinguish that fire.

He was frightened ***too*** much ***to*** speak anything.

The Preposition

It is another Part of Speech craves for your attention. As usual, before delving deep into the discussion of this, we may better have a little understanding of it.

Preposition is a word which is placed sometimes before and sometimes after a noun or pronoun to indicate, describe or show the relation of the said noun or pronoun with other words in the sentence.

She is walking slowly *on* the road.

The dog jumped *over* the gate.

Rony is writing *on* the paper *with* a pen.

There is no ink *in* the bottle.

In the above examples 'on', 'over', 'with' and 'in' are prepositions.

All the time the object does not bear the superiority of the preposition before it and sometimes force it to follow the object. The following are the compelling circumstances that a preposition should follow the object or be placed at the end of the sentence.

When the relative pronoun of a sentence is *'that'*, the preposition should be placed at the end of the sentence.

He is the man *that* you are looking *for*.

When a sentence is introduced with an interrogative pronoun, the preposition should be placed at the end of the sentence.

What you are searching *for*?

Where she is going *on*?

Despite their grunting, grudging and snarling, the prepositions *for, from, in, on* are banned before nouns of place or time. That means you should not use *for, from, in, on* before nouns of place or time.

All this happened last month.

We reached the playground quickly.

According to their form, nature and usage, Prepositions also are divided into several categories

Simple Prepositions:

In, off, by, at, for, from, on, through, with, up, to, till, with, are called as simple prepositions.

Compound Prepositions

By adding a simple letter or letters before a noun, adjective or adverb, compound prepositions are formed. The following are some of the examples.

Along, across, amidst, among, around, beside, etc.

Phrase prepositions:

Group of words which can be used as prepositions are called as phrase prepositions

In accordance with

According to

In addition to

The culprit shall be punished *in accordance with* law.

According to which he has got that courage I cannot understand.

In addition to these you have to take those papers also with you.

Some words sometimes used as prepositions and sometimes as adverbs. When a word is not commanding a noun or pronoun it is an adverb.

Don't loiter *about* (adverb)

It is *about* two feet long (preposition)

You have to be here *before* (adverb)

I will be there *before* long (preposition)

When the objects are relative pronouns, they shall be omitted after prepositions.

This is the pen I want to buy (*'what'* relative object for pen is omitted here)

<u>The prepositions 'in' and 'at':</u>

We use *'in'* when we are talking about places in broad and general sense

I have been residing *in* Kolkata for a long time.

We play football *in* playground

When we mean inside we use in:

She is *in* the house now.

It is *in* the pot.

With names of lanes

He is living in Cockroach lane

When we make a place particular, we have to use *'at'*

We stop at the playground while we are going to home.

Kolkata is a town where we can stop at to see and enjoy.

With house numbers, etc. at can be used

Ranjani arrived at house no.36

At can be used for point of time

He promised me to meet *at* evening.

They may arrive *at* 11 in the night

In can be used for a period of time.

I complete writing this book *in* this year itself.

Rony may arrive *in* this week itself.

When you used two places in a sentence, at should be used for the smaller one and in should be used for the bigger one.

He lived *at* Flowers Street *in* Chennai

<u>Preposition 'on':</u>

When we mean above we use *'on'*

The book is on the table.

<u>Preposition 'till':</u>

Preposition 'till' is used for time

You have to work *'till'* dark

Till 9.00 p.m. I stay there

<u>Preposition 'since':</u>

'Since' is used for *'point of time'*

He has been working in that school *since* 1999

Rony has been there *since* last year.

Since is used to *'indicate reason'*

Since you have studied hard, you qualified in the examination.

Since Rony has not arrived yet, I decided to leave this place.

Since he *had* no means, I have to support him in those days.

Since must always be followed by a verb in Perfect Tense *had, has* or *have*. So one thing logically here has to be understood is; *since* can be used relating to the past only

Preposition 'for':

'for' is used for *'period of time'*.

I have been working as an English teacher *for* more than fifteen years.

He is suffering like that *for* three years.

From

The privilege that has been given to *'from'* is; it can be used indicating past, present and future also.

She has been working in our home *from* two years.

From now on we shall play in that tournament.

From tomorrow onwards I do teach English to you.

Beside

The meaning of 'beside' is by the side of. The meaning of 'besides' is in addition to. By observing the following examples, you can get clarity.

The horse stood *beside* the cart.

The mango fruit has fallen *beside* the rock.

Besides mathematics, he agreed to teach us English also.

Besides prose, this book contains poems also.

Besides fever, he got cough also.

Conjunction

Conjunctions are used to join sentences or words. Conjunctions mostly do the duty of joining sentences or words.

Observe the following sentences:

Nikhil is tall **and** Williams is short

Slate **and** pencil

In the above examples **and** is the conjunction.

There are some pair conjunctions to which you have to pay attention. These conjunctions are also called as Correlative Conjunctions. These Correlative Conjunctions should be placed immediately before the words they qualify.

Either ....or

Either by bus *or* by train you can reach there.

Either by pen *or* by pencil he can write that.

Neither.......nor

Neither he *nor* his wife is generous

Neither Ranjan *nor* Sumukh knows about the new developments.

Not only........but also

(i) *Not only* he surprised *but also* became very happy

(ii) *Not only* he *but* his wife *also* is a doctor

(iii) *Not only* I became prosperous *but* I became knowledgeable *also.*

In the above (ii) and (iii) examples '*also*' used with a distance from '*but*' to give more proper sense.

<u>**Compound conjunctions:**</u>

If we use a phrase to connect words or sentences, we call it a Compound Conjunction. Phrase means just a group of words.

The notice was published in the news paper *so that* all people can know about it.

He made the people stand in queue *in order to* make the distribution easier.

Conjunctions are also divided into different categories

Coordinating Conjunctions:

The conjunctions which are used to join the sentences of same status and equality are called as Coordinating Conjunctions

Nikhil is a doctor *and* his wife is a professor

Neither has he known about it *nor* his wife.

Cumulative Conjunctions:

These conjunctions are also called as *Copulative Conjunctions*. These conjunctions just do the duty of adding two sentences. Too lazy to do any more than that.

Ratan is a boy *and* Lata is a girl.

The pen is on the table *and* the book is in the drawer.

Adversative Conjunctions:

These conjunctions are used to express the opposite or contrast.

This is a Sunday *but* we have to work in our office.

She is black in colour *but* appearing quite attractive.

Alternative Conjunctions:

These conjunctions are also called as *disjunctive conjunctions*. These conjunctions offer an alternative.

You may take either this road or that.

You can take rest in this room or in that hotel

The balloon may burst or the air may just leak out.

Illative conjunctions:

These conjunctions are used to express suppositions and assumptions

There might have been a downpour because of that all the crop drowned in the water.

The food might have been undercooked as such they did not like it at all

You might have scolded them otherwise they did not get angry

Subordinating Conjunction:

When a conjunction adds a dependent or unfinished sentence to the main sentence it is called as *Subordinating Conjunction.*

Please wait here *until* he comes.

Nikhil feels lot of surprise *when* he sees this.

Ranjan doesn't know *where* she is going.

In the above examples *until, when* and *where* are subordinating conjunctions.

Usually the following words are used as *subordinating conjunctions.*

Though, although, till, before, after, because, if, that, unless, when, where, as, while.

Subordinating conjunctions also can be divided into following categories:

Subordinating conjunctions of time:

These conjunctions introduce those subordinate sentences which indicate *point of time.*

Till he comes, I don't go away from here.

Mary shall be here *before* he comes.

The show will not begin *till* 9.00 p.m.

In the above examples *till* and *before* are Subordinating Conjunctions of Time.

Subordinating conjunctions of cause:

These conjunctions introduce those subordinate sentences which indicate *cause or reason* for something.

The glass broke into pieces *because* he hit it with his hand with such force.

Since he has studied hard, he sure gets good marks.

In the above examples *because* and *since* are Subordinating Conjunctions of Cause or Reason.

These conjunctions are called as ***Subordinating conjunctions of reason*** also

Subordinating conjunctions of purpose:

These conjunctions introduce those subordinate sentences which indicate *purpose* for something.

Nikhil is studying very hard *so as* to get good marks in his exams.

Mary is on strict diet *because* she wants to decrease her weight.

In the above examples *so as* and *because* are Subordinating Conjunctions of Purpose.

Subordinating conjunctions of result:

These conjunctions introduce those subordinate sentences which indicate *the result* or *consequence* for something.

Nikhil ate so much *that* he cannot stand from where he sat.

Rose wrote the examination very good *so that* she got first rank in her school.

In the above examples *that* and *so that* are Subordinating Conjunctions of Result.

These conjunctions are called as ***Subordinating conjunctions of consequence*** also

Subordinating conjunctions of condition:

These conjunctions introduce those subordinate sentences which require a *condition* to be fulfilled to get something.

Nikhil has to study hard *if* he wants to qualify in the examination.

Rose has to go by flight *if* she wants to reach there fast.

You have to go by bus *if* you want to spend less.

In the above examples *if* is the Subordinating Conjunctions of Condition.

Subordinating conjunctions of Concession:

These conjunctions introduce those subordinate sentences which gives a concession.

Though he is just a boy, he is allowed to participate in the games.

Though her poetry is not that much good, it is considered for prize.

In the above examples ***though*** is the Subordinating Conjunction of Concession.

<u>Subordinating conjunctions of Comparison:</u>

These conjunctions introduce those subordinate sentences which make comparisons.

Rose is clever ***than*** Sita (is)

Nikhil got good marks in his social exam ***than*** in his English exam

In the above examples ***than*** is the Subordinating Conjunction of Comparison.

You have to carefully examine whether a word is used as a conjunction or preposition as certain words can be used as both.

Wait ***till*** he comes. (preposition)

You wait here ***till*** he comes. (conjunction)

Nikhil is not here ***since*** last week. (preposition)

Since all the mangoes have been spoiled, we threw them away (conjunction)

When ***since*** is used as a ***preposition*** or ***conjunction*** it need not be followed by perfect tense.

Interjection

It is the smallest, simplest and tiniest of the Parts of Speech. To its utmost frustration, it has no capacity whatsoever to influence a sentence. It is just placed before a sentence and it remains there frustrated, helpless and emotionally spent up.

Hurrah! He made it once again!

Alas! He lost his last penny also.

Oh! She is pretty.

In the above examples *Hurrah! Alas!* and *Oh!* are Interjections.

Another important point: We have to use an exclamation mark '!' after an interjection

Hurrah! We need a celebration. We have just completed the Parts of Speech. There are only some more important things in English grammar that we need to discuss here.

Direct Speech and Indirect Speech

If we say something, as the person saying it himself, it is called as in Direct Speech. If what he has said is just reported, it is called as in Indirect Speech. Indirect Speech is called as Reported Speech also.

Ranga said "don't go there. It is dangerous" (Direct Speech)

Ranga cautioned us not to go there because it is dangerous. (Indirect Speech)

There are some rules which have to be followed while converting Direct Speech into Indirect Speech

The sentence in quotations can be called as main sentence. The sentence introducing the main sentence can be called as Subordinate Sentence.

Usually, in the Indirect Speech the main sentence shall be introduced by *that*.

Raju said "I never went there."

Raju said *that* he never went there.

If the subordinate sentence is in past tense, all the present tenses in the main sentence should be changed into corresponding past tense.

Raju said "I *am feeling* very well now."

Raju said that he *was feeling* very well then.

Nikhil said "Only Rakul *sees* picture."

Nikhil said that only Rakul *saw* the picture.

If the verb in the main sentence is '*shall*', it transforms into '*should*'.

Ranjan said "I *shall* go there."

Ranjan said that he *should* go there.

If the verb in the main sentence is *'will'*, it transforms into *'would'*.

I said "I *will* go there."

I said that I *would* go there.

If the main sentence is conveying an ever present truth it remains the same all the time even in whatever tense the subordinate sentence may be in.

Raju said "Sea water always tastes salty."

Raju said that sea water always tastes salty.

If the subordinate sentence is in present tense, the tense in the main sentence does not change at all.

He says, "She comes at any moment now."

He says that she comes at any moment now.

Raju says, "Mamatha went there yesterday".

Raju says that Mamatha went there yesterday.

Kamal is saying "I will go there tomorrow"

Kamal is saying that he will go there tomorrow..

She says "I want a mango now."

She says that she wants a mongo now

The pronouns in the main sentence should be changed according to the pronouns in the subordinate sentence.

He said "I study medicine."

He said that he would study medicine.

She said "I never worry about unnecessary things."

She said that she never worries about unnecessary things.

In the above examples the pronoun in the main sentence *'I'* in the direct speech was changed into *'he'* and *'she'* according to the pronoun in the subordinate sentence.

Usually the words expressing nearness in time and place shall change into the words expressing distance.

Nikhil said "*These* mangoes are very sweet."

Nihil said that *those* mangoes were very sweet.

Rose said "*This* red pen is very good to write."

Rose said that *that* red pen is very good to write.

Hariharan said "I do it *this* moment itself."

Hariharan said *that* he would do it that moment itself.

Mary said "*These* moments are very precious to me."

Mary said that *those* moments were very precious to her.

Williams said "I *shall* be here again by next week"

Williams said that he *should* be there again by next week

Ranga said "She is coming *here*."

Ranga said that she was coming *there*.

If it has been said at the same time or at the same place or subordinate sentence is in present tense, the tense of the verb in main sentence does not change. *That, this, these, those, here, there,* etc. words also do not change.

Nikhil says "*These* mangoes are very sweet."

Nihil says that *these* mangoes are very sweet.

Rose is saying "*This* red pen is very good to write."

Rose is saying that *this* red pen is very good to write.

Hariharan is saying "I do it *this* moment itself."

Hariharan is saying that he does it *this* moment itself.

Mary says that "*These* moments are very precious to me."

Mary says that *these* moments are very precious to her.

Ranga is saying "She is coming *here*."

Ranga is saying that she is coming *here*.

Kamal says "I want that book now."

Kamal says that he wants that book now.

Rony is saying "I will go there."

Rony is saying that she will go there.

Mani says "Those mangoes are very sweet."

Mani says that those mangoes are very sweet.

If the adverb *'yesterday'* is used in Direct Speech it should be changed into the *'day before'* in Indirect Speech. *Here* in Direct Speech shall be changed into *there* in Indirect Speech.

He said "I was here yesterday"

He said that he was there the day before.

'*Tomorrow*' in Direct Speech should be changed into '*the next day*' in Indirect Speech

He said "I shall be here tomorrow also."

He said that he should be there the next day also.

Some more important aspects in English Grammar

Congratulations! You have known English grammar in a comprehensive way. I did not say each and everything about grammar but I hope that I introduced all important aspects of English grammar and made you get an idea on it.

After knowing the following also, you can become even more proficient and skillful in English grammar.

The forms of 'Be':

Am, is are, was, were, be, being, are called as '*be*' forms. You already know that *am, is are, was, were* are used as verbs. There are other uses also to these. Along with *be, being* these words are used in forming passive voice.

I am taking the book with me (active voice)

The book *is being* taken with me (passive voice)

He tells me (Active Voice)

I *am* told by him. (Passive Voice)

He tells them (Active Voice)

They *are* told by him. (Passive Voice)

He took the ball with him. (Active Voice)

The ball *was* taken by him. (Passive Voice)

They took the bags with them (Active Voice)

The bags *were* taken by them (Passive Voice)

They were taking the bags with them. (Active Voice)

The bags were *being* taken with them. (Passive Voice)

They are taking the bags with them (Active Voice)

The bags are *being* taken with them (Passive Voice)

He shall take the book (Active Voice)

The book shall *be* taken by him. (Passive Voice)

Have, has

Other than verbs, the words *have, has* are used to indicate possession.

I *have* five pens with me.

She *has* no means to live.

By adding *'to'* to have and has we can indicate an obligation.

She *has to* write the examination to be qualified for the job.

You *have to* respect your elders.

Have sometimes used as a noun also by simple changes to it.

Haves (rich people)

Have- nots (poor people)

Had to

The word *had to* is used for the past obligation or compulsion.

I *had to* go there myself.

He *had to* become a servant in that house.

The uses of 'do', 'did':

To accentuate or press something:

I *do* it. Don't worry.

I *did* it with my own hands.

If we use *'do'* after a noun in third person singular form in simple present tense, *-es* should be added to it. Then no *–s* should be added to the other verb in the sentence if there is one.

He *does* it to prove himself.

Rose *does* it neither properly nor correctly.

'Do' generally means the ability to do something. So it is used in the questions like this.

Can you do it?

This pen do.

The word 'did'

'Did' is past tense of the auxiliary verb *'do'*. It is used in past tense for the same purposes of *'do'*.

I did it.

One very important point here. **Did** must always be followed by a verb in present tense.

I **did** learn English there.

Can

The word *'can'* is used to express ability in the present.

I **can** do that.

They never **can** do it.

Can sometimes be used to give permissions

You **can** go now

Could

The word *'could'* is used to express ability in the past. It may be surprising to you but **could** should always be followed by a verb in present tense

They **could** do that just in five minutes.

May

May tells us about a possibility in the present time.

He **may** come at any moment now.

It **may** cost twenty rupees.

May can be used in giving permission also.

You **may go** now.

Might

'Might' tells us about a possibility in the past time. *'Might'* should be followed by a verb in present tense

He **might** do that.

Rose **might** give the book to him.

Shall

'Shall' is used after second and third person pronouns to indicate commands, promises and threats.

You **shall** not take my book again (command)

You sure *shall* take my book tomorrow (promise)

The bomb *shall* explode at any moment (threat)

Will

'*Will*' is used with the first person for the following

To express a desire or decision.

I *will* carry my bag tomorrow.

We *will* carry our bags tomorrow.

To indicate habits

I *will* watch movies for any length of time.

He *will* consume tobacco all the time.

To guesses and possibilities

I hope he *will* do it good.

I think he *will be* the person you want to meet.

Other uses of 'will'

For requests

Will you borrow that book for me?

For invitations

Will you come to our home on next Monday?

Would

To indicate future in the past.

He said on that day that he *would* go to Goa next week.

To ask questions sometimes

If I say something *would* you mind?

Would you be here on next Monday?

For the plans of future which may happen or may not happen or possibilities of future

I *would* go to Mexico next week (I may go or may not go)

I am thinking that the balloon *would* burst at any moment (it may or may not)

Should

For obligations and duties

You *should* honor your country

You *should* maintain your timings

Must

Must is used for strong requirements

You *must* be qualified in the physical test otherwise you can't get the job

You *must* break the lock otherwise you cannot enter into the house

Ought to

Ought to also is used for duties, obligations and necessities

You *ought to* understand the circumstances

You *ought to* give respect to expect the same from others

Used to

Used to is used - to indicate habits in the past or something usually taking place in the past

I *used to* go there on every Sunday

He *used to* smoke cigarettes excessively

It used to rain everyday in the evening last week.

Need

Need is used to indicate necessities and takes 's' for third person singular in simple present tense

You *need* to go there to know about it.

He *needs* to study hard to qualify in the examination for his promotion.

Other Noteworthy Things

The formation of questions:

You have to put the verb in the beginning and subject after that in addition to keep the question mark in the end of a sentence to make a question.

He is honesty.

Is he honesty?

She is beautiful.

Is she beautiful?

He will come.

Will he come?

We can use 'Do' and 'Did' also to form questions. Observe the following sentences.

Do you know about it?

Does he know about it?

If the question is in simple present tense the '-es' should be added to 'Do' but not the verb.

Did she come then?

Did Lalit choose carams to play?

Just remember! While forming questions, you should not forget to give preference to the verb and put it in the beginning of the sentence. However much great the 'subject' is and comes most of the times at the beginning of the sentence, here they have to agree to verb to come before them like that.

Another important thing I almost forgot to tell! Never use a verb in the past tense after the verb 'Did'. I really cannot understand why grammarians developed love like that on present tense verbs that after some words like 'Did, Might, Could' you should use only a verb in present tense. Observe the following sentences.

Did he come to the festival?

Might he go there then?

Could she win in that race?

She did not know about it at that time.

A simple caution! Don't place '-s' after the verb.

Some other caution for you. Don't use two negatives in a sentence. Your intention may be to make the meaning very much negative but the sentence shall become positive and gives positive meaning.

He could not unable to achieve his goal.

Your intention may be to give more stressing to the meaning he could not achieve his goal but by using two negatives like that the meaning changes into 'He achieved his goal.' So simply say like this.

He could not achieve his goal.

Or

He was not able to achieve his goal.

You already came to know about 'either – or' and 'neither –nor' which can be used as conjunctions. The words 'either' and 'neither' only also can be used as adjectives in the following manner.

Either girl is ready to do it.

That means there are two girls at that moment there and both of them are ready to do it.

Neither pen is here.

That means there should have been two pens there but no pen is available at that moment.

Just remember! Either and neither should be followed only by a verb in singular.

Sometimes the same word can be used as an adjective and pronoun also. Only by observing the sentence you can know about it.

Which is the pen you are going to use?

Above 'which' is used as an interrogative pronoun.

Which pen you like the most?

In the above sentence 'which' is used as an adjective.

Sometimes 'this, that, these, those' can be used as demonstrative adjectives or demonstrative pronouns in a sentence. In such situation you can say whether those words are demonstrative adjectives or demonstrative pronouns by the usage of them in the said sentence.

This is Jhansi's dog. (Here 'this' is a demonstrative pronoun)

This dog is Jhansi's (Here 'this' is demonstrative adjective)

That is the book written by me. (Here 'that' is a demonstrative pronoun)

That book is written by me. (Here 'that' is a demonstrative adjective)

These are good mangoes to eat. (Here 'these' is a demonstrative pronoun)

These mangoes are good to eat. (Here 'these' is demonstrative adjective)

Those are the books bought by me. (Here 'those' is a demonstrative pronoun)

Those books are bought by me. (Here 'those' is demonstrative adjective)

'Which, what' can be used either as 'interrogative adjectives' or 'interrogative pronouns' also in a sentence. In which way they are used can be understood by the usage of them in a sentence.

Which pen you prefer to buy now? (Interrogative adjective)

Which is the pen you prefer to buy now? (Interrogative pronoun)

What picture you are going to draw in that competition? (Interrogative adjective)

What is the picture you are going to draw in that competition? (Interrogative pronoun)

The words **'Each, every, either and neither'** can be used either as demonstrative adjectives or demonstrative pronouns. We can determine them as adjectives or pronouns only by the usage of them in a sentence. In the following sentences these are used as adjectives.

Each boy took his book into his hands to read.

Every person respects his nation respects his judiciary also.

Either road leads to that destination.

Neither boy has the capacity to do it.

Even when they are used as adjectives all the pronouns that follow should be in singular and the verb also should be in singular.

In the following sentences **'Each, either and neither'** are used as pronouns.

Each of the mangoes you gave is sour.

Either of the way we take leads to that destination.

Neither of those comes here on this day

The nouns which follow the Distributive Pronouns must be in singular and should be followed by a verb in singular.

Could

'Could' can be used to say about ability but not performance of something.

He knew that he *could* write that essay.

But when he completed writing that essay, it should be said

He *was able to* write that essay.

But when we say things in a negative way, we can use either *'could not'* or *'was not able to'*.

He *could not* write that essay.

He *was not able* to write that essay.

Little, a little, the little

There is difference in the meaning of above three words. *'Little'* gives an absolute negative meaning, *'a little'* gives somehow positive meaning, *'the little'* gives confirmed positive meaning

Little furniture was left by those people when they left the house

The above sentence means no furniture has been left in that house.

Only *a little* furniture was left by those people when they left the house

The above sentence means small and negligible amount of furniture has been left.

The little furniture that has been left by those people came good help to us.

The above sentence means, some furniture has been left in that house and it became quite useful to the people residing in that house.

In the similar manner *few*, *a few* and *the few* also can be used.

Means:

Means can be used either in singular or plural. When it is used as an agent or instrument, it can be either singular or plural. But when it is used to give the meaning of wealth it should only be plural.

We can succeed in this mission by *this means* or *that means*.

We can succeed in this mission by *these means* or *those means*.

The *means* we have to overcome this difficulty *are* not many.

The superlative most

The superlative *most* sometimes used only to emphasize or give more prominence to something rather than to compare. This type of usage is called *superlative of eminence* or *absolute superlative.*

The most gracious thing!

The most vulgar speech!

Better to use an exclamation after the phrases.

If we wish to compare two qualities in the same person, we should not use –er comparative. We need to make such comparisons in the following manner.

Nathan is more brave than intelligent

Later, latest:

Later, latest refer to time.

We discuss about this *later*.

What is the *latest* news?

Latter, last:

Latter, last refer to position.

The person who stood *latter* in the que may not get the meals.

The *last* stone is not removed from the ground yet.

Usage of adjectives as nouns:

Sometimes adjectives can be used as nouns also in the following manner.

The rich should help *the poor*

The brave always win in the race.

In generous gesture, as nouns allowed adjectives to be used as nouns, adjectives allowed nouns also to be used as adjectives on some occasions.

The *red hat* man came to me in the evening.

The *bungalow* owner gave his bungalow on rent.

Some

'*Some*' is used to give positive and affirmative meaning.

He has *some* knowledge in carpentry and that shall certainly be helpful to him.

It can be used to make requests:

Will you please give me *some* milk?

It can be used to make offers:

Do you have *some* coffee?

Any

'*Any*' generally is used to give some negative meaning.

Do you have *any* manners at all? (Means he has no manners at all)

They did not leave *any* milk in the pot. (Means no milk has been left in the pot)

Sometimes to give a positive meaning also.

Any person can do that.

If there are *any* oranges available in the market, I shall buy some.

Possessive adjectives & possessive pronouns:

My, our, your, his, her, their are called as possessive adjectives as they do the duty of the adjectives being attached to nouns.

My pen, our car, your bag, his hat, her book, their house

They can do the work of a possessive pronouns also with little change in them.

My book is on the table. (Here *my* is possessive adjective)

The book on the table is *mine*. (Here my transformed into *mine* to become a possessive pronoun.)

We kept *our* bags in the last room. (Here *our* is possessive adjective)

The bags which are kept in the last room are *ours* (Here we need to add *–s* to *our* to make it a possessive pronoun)

I have *your* mobile with me (Here *your* is possessive adjective)

The mobile I have with me is *yours.* (Here also we need to add *–s* to your to make it a personal pronoun)

His hat is in yellow color (Here *his* is possessive adjective)

The *hat* in yellow color is his. (Here *his* is possessive pronoun)

When singular noun and plural noun joined together, the plural noun should come later and the verb must agree with the plural noun.

The teacher and the students left their places.

Neither the mother nor the children took their meals.

Either he or his colleagues forgot to tell this to their boss

Antecedent

The subject, which the relative pronoun refers, is called as the antecedent of that relative pronoun. An antecedent is so much important and it must be present in almost all the sentences.

He who studies hard will pass in the examination.

The mangoes that are kept on the table, meant for you.

The joke that he cut did not make the people laugh.

In the above examples, the subjects 'he', 'the mangoes' and 'the joke' are called as the antecedents of the relative pronouns 'who' and 'that'

Omission of antecedent

However much important, this antecedent also sometimes gets bore and wants to take rest. Such occasions are not many but then it gives the privilege to the relative pronoun to be present at the beginning of the sentence and the antecedent disappears from it. Observe the following sentences:

Who goes on that way, goes easily.

Whoever meet me on this day, gets one hundred rupees.

If we elaborate the above sentences

He who goes on that way, goes easily

He whoever meets me on this day, gets one hundred rupees

In the above sentences, the antecedent, the subject 'he' is omitted.

Agreement of the verb with the antecedent

Antecedent does not approve any disobedience from the verb. The verb must be of the same number and person of the antecedent. And the pronoun that follows the antecedent also should be in singular.

He who works hard succeeds in his life

Here 'he' the subject is in singular. So the verb 'works' and 'succeeds' should be in singular. And the pronoun 'his' that follows also is in singular.

Those who work hard succeed in their life.

Here as the subject 'those' is in plural, the verbs 'work' and 'succeed' also should be in plural. And the pronoun 'their' that follows also should be in singular.

Transitive verbs & intransitive verbs

A verb is called as transitive if it denotes an action that passes from the subject to the object. That means, if a sentence has a transitive verb it should have a subject and object also. Most of the transitive verbs satisfy themselves with a single object. Observe the following examples.

He ate a mango.

Lata did her homework.

Jwalan went to school.

But some transitive verbs are not like that and they need more, another object also. Ask, give, take, are the verbs of this sort.

He asked me a rupee

I gave a mango to him

Raju gave the cycle to Lata.

In the above examples 'me', 'a mango' and 'cycle' are called as indirect objects and 'a rupee', 'him' and 'Lata' as direct objects.

Dative case

When a sentence has two objects as above said, the two objects it has called as 'direct object' and 'indirect object'. Observe the following examples:

Lata gave a book to Rajani

Sadan gave some coins to the beggar

In the above two sentences 'a book' and 'some coins' are indirect objects and 'Rajani' and 'the beggar' are direct objects. What things further you noticed? The indirect object should come immediately after the verb and before the direct object. Don't think as it is indirect object has not been given much importance and can be thrown to the end of the sentence. The 'direct object' however much it bubbles with anger, it should stay at the end of the sentence.

When a sentence is like in the above, it is said to be in the dative case. Another important thing, I will forget if I don't tell about it here itself. You can make dative case only with 'the transitive verbs.'

The other noticeable thing here is; as the dative case is only for the transitive verbs, the sentences in dative case can be made into passive. We shall try that also.

The passive voice for the first sentence above mentioned:

A book was given to Rajani by Lata.

Some coins were given to the beggar by Sadan.

If the 'direct object' is feeling too much as it has been given only the next place even in passive also, we can make them pacified in the following manner. That means; we can make the passive voice sentences in this way also by making the direct object stand at the beginning of the sentence.

Rajani was given a book by Lata.

The beggar was given some coins by sadan.

When the object has become the subject in passive voice the verb that follows it should agree with its number and person. As the 'Rajani' and 'the beggar' were singular pronouns, the singular verb 'was' followed it.

It may be an insult to the subjects in active voice but they would be thrown to the end of the sentences and made as objects when a sentence is transformed into passive from active.

Some verbs have a privilege that they can be used either *transitively* or *intransitively* also. You can say whether they are transitive or intransitive verbs only by the usage of them in a sentence. Observe the following examples.

He *fought* with me yesterday (transitive)

I have never seen him *fighting* (intransitive)

(You) swim back to the shore (transitive)

She *swam* quickly (intransitive)

However much they are restricted, some intransitive verbs cannot refrain themselves without being used as transitive. So they have been given the facility to be used as transitive in the following manner.

He *walks* fast (intransitive)

The baby *walks* with him. (transitive)

The horse *runs* slowly because it is wounded. (intransitive)

He *runs* a shop to eke out his livelihood. (transitive)

Some intransitive verbs have been given the facility to be used as transitive but they must allow some change in them. Observe the following examples.

Exhausted fully, he *fall* on the ground (intransitive)

He make the stone *fell* on the ground (transitive)

Here the intransitive verb *'fall'* has been made to *'fell'* to be used as transitive.

Lie where you are (intransitive)

You *lay* the mango on the table (transitive)

Here the intransitive verb *'lie'* has been made to *'lay'* to be used as transitive.

I *rise* from the bed early in the morning (intransitive)

Raise the rice sack from the table and put it in the cart (transitive)

Here the intransitive verb *'rise'* has been made to *'raise'* to be used as transitive.

Sit calmly without making noise (intransitive)

You *set* it right on the ground (transitive)

Here the intransitive verb *'sit'* has been made to *'set'* to be used as transitive.

Some intransitive verbs have been allowed to be used as transitive verbs if they allow a preposition beside them. Observe the following examples.

However many times we *talk about* it, we cannot solve it.

I don't intend to *run at* risk at this moment.

He always *laughs at* poor people.

I hope he will *look into* that problem as soon as possible.

You *asked for* it and I gave it to you.

Cognate object or cognate accusative

However much banned, sometimes intransitive verbs dare themselves to take an object but that object has the meaning just like the verb. Observe the following examples.

The military did not *fight* a good *fight*.

The baby *dreamt* a horrifying *dream*.

She never *sleeps* the *sleep* of peace.

You *live* the *life* of worthy

Here the object has the meaning similar to the verb so it is called as *'cognate object'* or *'cognate accusative'.*

Adverbial adjective or adverbial accusative

If a noun is used with a verb, an adverb or an adjective to define it even more, it is called as adverbial adjective or adverbial accusative.

I stayed there one *hour* full.

She went *park* for time pass.

The iron weighs ten *kilograms.*

The transitive verbs also have the desire to be used in the other way, as intransitive verbs without considering it as inferior. It is allowed in the following manner.

The thieves *burnt* the house after stealing the things in it (transitive)

The house *burnt* itself in the fire (intransitive)

I never expected that he would *break* his promise (transitive)

He *broke* his courage on seeing that (intransitive)

<u>Verb of incomplete predication & complement of the verb</u>

An intransitive verb does not need an object, okay, but can an intransitive verb gives the full meaning without attaching anything to it? Not all intransitive verbs have that capacity. Some intransitive verbs must be followed by something to give complete meaning. Just observe the following examples.

Having that praise from his boss he *seems happy.*

If you don't put the word *'happy'* after the verb *'seems'* in the above sentence, it would not give full meaning.

Without having collected his rents, the land owner *appeared angry.*

Without the word *'angry'* after the verb *'appeared'*, the above sentence would not give full meaning.

Such verbs which have no capacity to give full meaning without some attachment to them are called as *verbs of incomplete predication.* The words or attachments to such verb to help it give full meaning are called as *complement of the verb* or *complement of the predicate.*

In the examples of above sentences the verbs *'seems'* and *'appeared'* are verbs of incomplete predication and the words 'happy' and 'angry' are *'complement of the verb'* or *'complement of the predicate'.*

These *complement of the verb* is may be a noun or an adjective also and it does the work of describing the noun. Therefore it is called as *subjective compliment.* If the ***complement of the verb*** is a noun, it will be called as ***predicative noun*** and if it is an adjective it will be called as ***predicative adjective***.

Observe the following examples.

The dog is black (here it is ***predicative adjective)***

Rama is the class leader (here it is ***predicative noun***)

When the ***subjective compliment*** is a noun it must be in the ***nominative case***

Objective compliment

Sometimes in addition to the object, the sentences with transitive verbs need a qualifier to the object to give full meaning and that qualifier is called as *'objective compliment'*.

Reading that book gave him ***lot of knowledge***

Donating money to the poor made him ***popular***

She called him ***a liar***

In the above sentences *'lot of knowledge'*, *'popular'* and *'a liar'* are objective compliments

Adjectives as Nouns and Nouns as Adjectives

It is indeed boring to play the same role all the time, is it is not? So the parts of speech in grammar also want variety. So sometimes 'adjectives' want to act as 'nouns' and 'nouns' want to act as 'adjectives'. Observe the following.

Adjectives as nouns:

'The brave' never do feel fear to any.

'The rich' do not know the hardships of *'the poor'*

In the end it is *'the mighty'* who win.

In the above sentences, brave, rich and poor are adjectives but used as nouns. Don't think they get the privilege alone. They have to take the help of the definite article 'the' to get this status. That means the definite article should be placed before these adjectives to make them cherish their desire to act as nouns.

This facility is not just to the adjectives. Certain nous also can be used as adjectives in the following manner.

American writer, Arabian horse, Asian culture

Here nouns America, Arabia and Asia are used as adjectives. They don't need the help of indefinite article 'the' to be used as adjectives but they just cannot be used in their general form. They have to allow some modification in themselves. In the above examples America turned into American, Arabia into Arabian and Asia into Asian.

But some nouns are too adamant to allow any change in them to be used as adjectives. But still they are allowed to act as adjectives. Observe the following examples.

Malaysia government, Thailand tourism.

Position of adjectives

When the adjectives are used attributively, it should be put immediately before the noun.

My uncle is a *kind* person

She has a *stone* heart.

When several adjectives are used to describe a noun more, they will be put after it to give more emphasis.

The man *with curly hair and black dress* went in this way just five minutes before.

I liked the girl *with rosy cheeks and white frock.*

Correct use of articles

Articles are in fact demonstrative adjectives. Unnecessary repetition of them change the meaning of the sentence.

Observe the following sentences.

Rosy has a blue and black notebook

The above sentence means that Rosy has a notebook and it is blue and black.

Rosy has a blue and a black notebook

The above sentence means that Rosy has two notebooks one is blue in colour and the other is black in colour.

Gerund and Present Participle

The same word can be used as either gerund or present participle. We can determine whether it is gerund or present participle only by the usage of it in a sentence. Anyhow it is indeed better to know what is gerund and what is present participle before doing any analysis on them.

Gerund

Gerund is a verbal noun. That means gerund occurs from a verb and do the duty of a noun. Observe the following words

Thinking, swimming, reading, jumping

Now observe the following sentences using the above words. These words are formed by adding *–ing* to the verbs *–think, -swim, -read* and *-jump*. If they used as nouns in the following sentences, they are called as *gerunds.*

'*Thinking*' was unknown to the primitive people

She could do '*swimming*' very fast.

Everyday '*reading*' English newspaper develops your English.

'*Jumping*' is one of the games we play in our school.

The following are the uses of a *gerund.*

It can be used as a subject of a sentence:

Swimming is the best exercise.

It can be used as an object of a sentence:

When we reached that place we found him *standing* on the ground

Just like some objects, it also wishes to be governed by a preposition while acting as an object.

I went to a movie to get rid of *boring*.

We need special clothing to learn the art of *swimming*

You have to go to library to develop the habit of *reading.*

The *gerund* can be used as a complement to a verb also.

It *is disgusting* to hear vulgarism

Seeing comedy movies *is amusing* to anyone.

Present Participle

Present participle is a verbal adjective. That means it occurs from a verb and do the duty of an adjective. We can consider the same above words for this purpose also.

Thinking, swimming, reading, jumping

I need not say, here present participle has been formed by adding *–ing* to the verbs *–think, -swim, -read* and *-jump.*

Thinking deep, he came to the opinion it is the right time to do it.

Swimming fast, he crossed that river just in one hour.

I could not finish *reading* of that book in one day.

While *jumping* over the wall, the dog wounded itself.

Present participle denotes a period of action that is or was going on. Even though it has the word present in it, it denotes an action that went on for a period of time in the past also and may happen for a period of time in future also.

I am afraid, by reading that book I may become mad.

By seeing that movie, they certainly do pass their time in the best way tomorrow.

Going by your cycle, you cannot reach there fast.

Besides present participle, there is past participle also. It also does the work of an adjective but in a different way. The third form of a verb is called as past participle and most of the past participles do form by adding –n, -en, or –ed to the present tense verb

Spent, built, burnt, earned, read

While present participle denotes something in progress, past participles denotes something that is completed. It can be used most conveniently only with past actions.

Houses *built* with mud, don't last long.

The money I *spent* was much but the result I got was little.

I *spent* nearly two hundred rupees to buy that book.

In addition to these past and present participles there is another participle also. That is perfect participle. These perfect participles do take shape by adding past participle to 'having'

Having done his duty, he went to his home in the evening.
Having lost everything, he went home empty handed.

The End

Don't miss out!

Visit the website below and you can sign up to receive emails whenever Kotra Siva Rama Krishna publishes a new book. There's no charge and no obligation.

https://books2read.com/r/B-A-ATOV-IMXEC

BOOKS2READ

Connecting independent readers to independent writers.

Did you love *English Grammar Simplifier*? Then you should read *Rose Garden*[1] by Kotra Siva Rama Krishna!

[2]

Jasmine who was a ninth class student has a weakness. She could not remain silent if any of her friends were suffering for anything. She would go to any extent and probe into their personal matters also even sometimes that got her into problems.

When Jasmine told by her friend Mounika that her parents were going to be divorced, Jasmine could not remain calm seeing her friend distressed. She promised to Mounika that she would see not only that her parents be together all the time but they love and like each other always and the three of them spend a happy future forever.

To keep her promise, what Jasmine did, what difficulties she faced whether she became successful or not is the main theme of this novel

---

1. https://books2read.com/u/b5jewp

2. https://books2read.com/u/b5jewp

'Rose Garden'. But this 'Rose Garden' is not just that. This 'Rose Garden' is the heartbeat of teenage children. How they feel, how they want their parents to be, how they want their teachers to be, how they want their life to be.

Also by Kotra Siva Rama Krishna

Two Strangers On The Bed
A Girl's Conflict
Enna
Strawberry
Dusk
Just Relax!
Delicious Predicament
Nirupama
Half Opened Doors
Lovenest
Moonshine
Scarecrow
Closed Doors
Disturbed
Handfuls of Sand
Mansion of Illusions
Rain Flower
Rose Garden
Sand Dunes
Snow Flower
Split Personality
Being Possessed
Objection Sustained
House of Delusions
Rustle in the Leaves

Sasikala
Amaswitha
English Grammar Simplifier
Wisps of Smoke
Shadow in the Mirror
Love is Dangerous with a Stranger
Shadow of a Spirit
Unwanted Guests
Broken Window
Loud Thunder Nearby
Spirit in the Mirror
Whispers in the Night
Shadows in the Twilight
Twisted Shadow
Body, Mind and You
Summer Holidays
Flower of the Mist
Nail Polish
Laughter of a Spirit
Lipstick
Flickering Shadow
Dancing Shadow